Dearth, public policy and social disturbance
in England, 1550–1800

New Studies in Economic and Social History

Edited for the Economic History Society by
Michael Sanderson
University of East Anglia, Norwich

This series, specially commissioned by the Economic History Society, provides a guide to the current interpretations of the key themes of economic and social history in which advances have recently been made or in which there has been significant debate.

In recent times economic and social history has been one of the most flourishing areas of historical study. This has mirrored the increasing relevance of the economic and social sciences both in a student's choice of career and in forming a society at large more aware of the importance of these issues in their everyday lives. Moreover specialist interests in business, agricultural and welfare history, for example, have themselves burgeoned and there has been an increased interest in the economic development of the wider world. Stimulating as these scholarly developments have been for the specialist, the rapid advance of the subject and the quantity of new publications make it difficult for the reader to gain an overview of particular topics, let alone the whole field.

New Studies in Economic and Social History is intended for students and their teachers. It is designed to introduce them to fresh topics and to enable them to keep abreast of recent writing and debates. All the books in the series are written by a recognised authority in the subject, and the arguments and issues are set out in a critical but unpartisan fashion. The aim of the series is to survey the current state of scholarship, rather than to provide a set of prepackaged conclusions.

The series has been edited since its inception in 1968 by Professors M. W. Flinn, T. C. Smout and L. A. Clarkson, and is currently edited by Dr Michael Sanderson. From 1968 it was published by Macmillan as *Studies in Economic History*, and after 1974 as *Studies in Economic and Social History*. From 1995 *New Studies in Economic and Social History* is being published on behalf of the Economic History Society by Cambridge University Press. This new series includes some of the titles previously published by Macmillan as well as new titles, and reflects the ongoing development throughout the world of this rich seam of history.

For a full list of titles in print, please see the end of the book.

Dearth, public policy and social disturbance in England, 1550–1800

Prepared for the Economic History Society by

R. B. Outhwaite
University of Cambridge

 CAMBRIDGE
UNIVERSITY PRESS

Published by the Press Syndicate of the University of Cambridge
The Pitt Building, Trumpington Street, Cambridge CB2 1RP
40 West 20th Street, New York, NY 10011-4211, USA
10 Stamford Road, Oakleigh, Melbourne 3166, Australia

© The Economic History Society 1991

Printed in Great Britain at the University Press, Cambridge

A catalogue record for this book is available from the British Library

Library of Congress cataloguing in publication data

Outhwaite, R. B.
    Dearth, public policy and social disturbance in England, 1550–1800 /
prepared for the Economic History Society by R. B. Outhwaite.
        p.   cm. – (New studies in economic and social history)
    First published 1991.
    Includes bibliographical references and index.
    ISBN 0 521 55273 7 (hc). – ISBN 0 521 55780 1 (pb)
    1. England – Economic conditions. 2. England – Social conditions.
3. Great Britain – Politics and government. I. Economic History Society.
II. Title. III. Series.
HG254.5.094   1995   95–18714
306'.0946–dc20   CIP

ISBN 0 521 55273 7 hardback
ISBN 0 521 55780 1 paperback

Contents

Acknowledgement

I wish to thank the Editor of this series, Professor Leslie Clarkson, for the encouragement he gave me at an early stage and for the critical advice offered later.

Note on references

References in the text within brackets relate to the items, and editions, listed alphabetically in the Select Bibliography. Page numbers, where deemed necessary, are in italics. Where an author has two publications in the same year, these are differentiated as a and b items.

1

The meaning and measurement of dearth

Introduction

The natural and economic crises at the centre of this study recurred in a country that over the 250 years from 1550 to 1800 was experiencing significant economic and social changes. At the start of this period the population of England was about 3 million and it was then growing. This expansion continued until a peak of nearly 5.3 million was reached in the later 1650s. Thereafter a fall in numbers occurred for about thirty years and although this was followed by some gentle growth, that peak of 5.3 million was not to be exceeded until 1717. A further, but short-lived, setback occurred in the years 1728–31, and it was not until the second half of the eighteenth century that growth rates generally overtook those of Elizabethan England. By 1801, however, the population of England stood at just under 8.7 million (Wrigley and Schofield, 1981, *208–9*).

These three phases – population growth to the later 1650s, a decline and recovery that amounted to overall stagnation in the following hundred years, and more vigorous growth from the middle of the eighteenth century – produced similar directional tendencies in the long-term movements of grain prices. In a society in which bread and beer figured prominently in common diets, movements in grain prices had important consequences for popular living standards. These were put under pressure by the price inflation of the first phase, relieved by the stagnation of grain prices that ensued from the 1650s to the 1740s, only to be pressured again by the rise that took place in the second half of the eighteenth century.

These interlocking changes in population levels, grain prices, and living standards are one set of developments to keep in mind. Others are the changing locational and occupational distributions of this population. Wrigley has estimated that in the 1520s around 5.5 per cent of the population of England lived in towns of more than 5000 inhabitants. By 1670, however, this proportion had grown to 13.5 per cent, a figure that was to double again to 27.5 per cent by 1801 (Wrigley, 1986, *140*). Although these benchmarks do not fit neatly with our previous periodisation, they do emphasise that one important development was the continual growth of town-dwelling (grain-consuming rather than grain-producing) populations. Food consumers increased more rapidly than food producers, a tendency that was accentuated in certain regions by the growth of mining, quarrying and manufacturing employments, but one which cannot be measured over the country as a whole with any pretence at precision. Mining and quarrying were not urban pursuits, and a good many of those employed in the expanding manufacturing sector were located in rural and small-town England rather than in the larger towns. Moreover, all three branches of activity flourished in agricultural regions that were more pastoral than arable in their agricultural leanings (Thirsk, 1961). Eighteenth-century industrial expansion increased the tendencies for regions such as the West and East Midlands, West Yorkshire and South Lancashire to be grain deficient, even in years of average yields, and thus to be reliant on supplies from other areas (Wells, 1988, *22*). It is against this changing backcloth that the drama of periodic dearth was enacted.

But what did 'dearth' mean?

Contemporary usages

'Scarcity which makes food dear': so ran the first of Dr Johnson's definitions of dearth in his dictionary of 1755, sensibly making high victual prices the outcome of supply deficiencies.[1] A century or so before this, however, it was common for scarcity and dearness to be coupled in a less functional manner. Thus Archbishop

[1] Samuel Johnson, *A Dictionary of the English Language* (2 vols, London, 1755).

Whitgift could write in 1595 of 'this Tyme of Scarcitye & Dearth of Corne and Victualls', whilst a correspondent in Dublin the following year reversed the order in reporting on 'the dearth and scarcity of corn and victuals . . . in the Pale'.[2] This rather indiscriminate coupling emphasises the independent contemporary meaning of dearth as severely enhanced prices.

Although the term could be applied to almost anything – fish, rabbits, butter and cheese, partridges and pheasants – dearth was usually reserved for sharp elevations in the prices of more basic products – bread and beer – and the grainstuffs from which they derived. When in sixteenth- and seventeenth-century England men spoke of dearth, they were commenting on the prices of these goods reaching alarmingly high levels, levels that were likely to have dangerous social, and perhaps political, consequences. Contemporary didactic literature and reports to government officers frequently invoked the spectres of famine, desperate poverty, disease and disorder. A funeral orator in January 1597 spoke of 'the heavens . . . continual weeping, the earth glutted with waters, into barrenness . . . the sword of the enemy abroad to threaten us, famine and fear of mortality at home . . .'. Two years before this, in September 1595, the Lord Mayor of London warned Lord Treasurer Burghley that grain shortages were such that 'a great number of poor people that wear sore pinched & very low brought by the extremity of the last year would be decayed & utterly undoon', leading to 'the like clamors of the poorer sort & other inconvenences' as had been seen before.[3]

Dearth, in the first half of our period, carried with it certain implications: the heightening of grain prices was associated with worsening poverty, perhaps leading to talk of famine; with reports of growing sickness and increasing mortality; and with fears of social unrest. It is perhaps no surprise that Francis Bacon should list 'dearth' amongst the 'causes and motives of sedition'.[4] This fear lurked constantly in the minds of the rulers of Tudor and early Stuart England, shaping their responses to these events.

From Restoration times onwards the term may have been less

[2] F. Peck, *Desiderata Curiosa* (1732) 1, lib V, pp. 7–8; *Calendar of State Papers, Ireland, 1592–96*, pp. 457–8.

[3] HMC *Frankland-Russell-Astley Mss*, p. 5; Corporation of London Records Office, *Remembrancia*, II, no. 104.

[4] O. Smeaton, *Essays of Francis Bacon* (London, 1906), p. 45

frequently employed by contemporary complainants, reporters and governments, though not by historians of the latter part of our period. Some aspects of the rhetoric of dearth fell away: there was less talk of famine and sickness and more emphasis upon purely economic hardships. Although Thompson can write, of the eighteenth century, 'Dearths were real dearths. High prices meant swollen bellies and sick children whose food was coarse bread made up from stale flour', the changing flavour of contemporary comment is well rendered in the remark that he also cites about the 'truly painful' rising prices of 1795. These, an observer noted, 'have stript the cloaths from their backs, torn the shoes and stockings from their feet, and snatched the food from their mouths' (Thompson, 1971, *134*).

But how can we identify these episodes? In which years was dearth a threat? We shall attempt to answer these questions by looking first at contemporary discussions of the causes of dearth, and secondly at the behaviour of grain prices.

Contemporaries and the causes of dearth

Many, perhaps most, contemporaries realised that the worst dearths were the product of severely depleted harvests, themselves the consequence of adverse weather conditions. Even Tudor and Stuart governments were at times forced to admit this, though rulers frequently offered alternative explanations, embracing fundamental sin and economic avarice, looking to cast the blame elsewhere in order to justify their administrative interventions (Walter and Wrightson, 1976, *28–34*). Some realism can be found, for example, in the royal proclamation of 16 September 1621 banning the export of grain. It complained that 'by reason of the cold and unseasonable weather, which hath beene of late, specially this summer time, the fruits of the earth, and chiefly Corne and graine, are not either for plenty or goodnesse answerable to former yeeres' so that prices were rising.[5] Generally, it can be said that the nearer one gets to the actual producers, rather than the consumers of grainstuffs, the more one finds such realism prevailing.

[5]   J. F. Larkin and P. L. Hughes (eds), *Stuart Royal Proclamations* (Oxford, 1973) 1, p. 521.

It is difficult, however, to offer neatly packaged climatic reasons for these harvest failures. For one thing diets varied regionally, and changes took place over time. At the start of our period wheat was the preferred bread corn of the relatively affluent throughout England, barley was the poor man's bread corn wherever it was grown in the Midlands and the South, whilst oatmeal fulfilled the same role over large parts of the North. By the later eighteenth century wheat had a place in the common man's diet to a much greater extent, though barley and oats retained their importance in the West and the North (Wells, 1988, *13–16*). Secondly, as Jones reminds us, times of sowing and other characteristics 'are not the same for wheat, barley, oats and other crops which are harvested' (Jones, 1964, *56*). Thus variations in soils, precipitation and temperature could produce different yields in different areas. Thirdly, farmers to some degree were able to adjust their sowings to counter adverse weather conditions: an early seasonal calamity, such as a cold and wet autumn and winter that inhibited the growth of autumn-sown wheat might, if the weather relented, lead to correspondingly larger acreages being put down to spring-sown barley and pulses (Jones, 1964, *56*). Thus an early seventeenth-century Devon man noted in November 1608 that 'An extreme dearth of corn happened this year, by reason of extreme frosts (as the like were never seen), the winter going before, which caused much corn to fall away; so that many did sow barley where their wheat was sown before, thinking their wheat would never come to good'.[6]

Prolonged cold and wet weather in the crucial autumn and spring germination periods could be fatal for annual grain yields, however, though some of the worst calamities appear to be associated with continual rainfall preceding and during the harvest months.

Some people, particularly in the sixteenth and seventeenth centuries, were inclined to see the heavy hand of God in these calamities, and none more so, of course, than those in clerical positions. 'The lord goeth out against us in the season which was wonderfull wett, flouds every weeke', wrote the gloomy Ralph Josselin, vicar of Earl's Colne, in June 1648, and by August he had

---

[6] B. W. Clapp, H. E. S. Fisher and A. R. J. Jurica (eds), *Documents in English Economic History* (1977) p. 49.

'retired my selfe to seeke to god by reason of his judgments on us'.[7] The role of the 'doctrine of judgements' in these events has been skilfully explored elsewhere (Walter and Wrightson, 1976). Put simply, God's 'three arrows' of 'plague, famine and sword' were the result of human sins. Consequently not only were gluttony, drunkenness, and avarice frequently invoked as ultimate causes of these calamities, but also the opportunity was taken by those in authority to extol the merits of the Christian virtues. So, on Christmas Day 1596, the Privy Council could argue that 'the heavie displeasure of God' had been brought about by the 'excesse in dyett', and the Archbishop of Canterbury was asked to instruct preachers to 'exhort men . . . to abstynence and praier, and to use all charitable devotion towards the releif of their poore neighbors both in housekeeping, setting them a worke, giving of almes and other charitable workes, and sparing other excessive and super-fluous expences of vyctualles'. The people must be instructed 'to indure this scarsety with patyence'.[8] Attempts were made also, as we shall note in chapter 3, to curb alternative uses for grains and pulses.

The 'doctrine of judgements' may have lost some of its persuasiveness as alternative explanations of natural phenomena were espoused in the Enlightenment, but it continued to be invoked. The horsemen of the apocalypse ride rampant through Malthus's first *Essay on the Principle of Population* (1798), as exemplified by passages such as this:

The vices of mankind are active and able ministers of depopulation. They are the precursors in the great army of destruction; and often finish the dreadful work themselves. But should they fail in this war of extermination, sickly seasons, epidemics, pestilence, and plague, advance in terrific array, and sweep off their thousands and ten thousands. Should success be still incomplete, gigantic inevitable famine stalks in the rear, and with one mighty blow levels the population with the food of the world.[9]

Governments also could still employ the old rhetoric. Take, for example, the following preamble to an 'official prayer' ordered to be preached from pulpits throughout the land:

[7] A. Macfarlane (ed.) *Diary of Ralph Josselin, 1616–1683* (1976) pp. 129–30.
[8] *Acts of the Privy Council, 1596–97*, pp. 383–5.
[9] T. R. Malthus, *An Essay on the Principle of Population*, A. Flew (ed.) (Harmondsworth, 1982) pp. 118–19.

For the removal of those heavenly judgements which our manifold sins and provocations have most justly deserved, and with which Almighty God is pleased to visit the iniquities of the land by a grievous scarcity and dearth of diverse articles of sustenance and necessaries of life . . .

It comes not from the sixteenth century, as the language perhaps suggests, but from the middle of the nineteenth century. It is the official prayer ordered to be proclaimed from pulpits throughout the land on 24 March 1847.[10]

Price behaviour

There are no adequate measures of the variations that actually occurred in gross and net yields of corn. No statistics of national production or marketing exist before the twentieth century. There are precious few records even of individual farm output and sales. We have to make do, therefore, with proxies, such as price behaviour. But as dearth signified itself to contemporaries mainly via price movements, this is no great loss. Dearth meant sharply rising prices, rises sufficient to produce cries of complaint and distress.

Some contemporaries, particularly in the late seventeenth century, tried to establish the precise relationships between variations in output and variations in prices. Charles Davenant, drawing upon the work of Gregory King, produced the following formula (Thirsk and Cooper, 1972, *814*), one which was subsequently reproduced, and sometimes reworked, by later writers (Creedy, 1986):

We take it, that a defect in the harvest may raise the price of corn in the following proportions:
Defect raises the price above the common rate.

1 tenth	3	tenths
2 ,,	8	,,
3 ,,	1.6	,,
4 ,,	2.8	,,
5 ,,	4.5	,,

[10] R. N. Salaman, *The History and Social Influence of the Potato* (Cambridge, 1949; reprinted 1970) p. 314.

What this suggests is that prices rose disproportionately more than the decreases that took place in the size of the harvest, a characteristic that economists have been inclined to explain in terms of an inelastic demand for bread grains.

One cannot, however, use prices to establish the size of the harvest for a number of reasons. One is that the King-Davenant set of quantum relationships is obscure in that we cannot be certain whether its authors were thinking in terms of gross yields or net yields. Farmers would not necessarily market all they produced; some grain might be consumed on the farm, or reserved for next year's seed. Wrigley, in an intriguing recent paper, has explored this ambiguity, showing how marketable quantities might have behaved if certain withdrawals were made by farmers for current fodder or future seed corn. If, as he suggests, the quantum best expresses the relationship between quantities marketed and price, then one has to admit this additional variable into the calculation (Wrigley, 1989). Not all that was marketed in a particular region was necessarily produced there; and not all that was produced in a region was necessarily marketed there. Moreover, not only could marketable quantities vary regionally, they might also vary over time. Although Wrigley is inclined to believe that seeding rates remained constant, the feeding of grains to livestock may well have been influenced by the increasing availability of alternative fodder crops as the period progressed. There is a reminder here that demands for grain were not totally inelastic and that they could vary over time. In the short run, events such as war could inflate demands for grains in particular regions in order to provision troops. In the long run, as has been argued, changes in dietary patterns take place.

As if these problems are not sufficient, we should also remember that the formulae might be different from one species of grain to the next. The Davenant quantum-set simply refers to 'corn'. Weather conditions would not hit all crops alike, and consumers might 'trade down' from more expensive to less expensive grains in dearth years. Prices would even vary between qualities of the same grain. Sir Henry Cock, Deputy Lieutenant of Hertfordshire, reported to Burghley in the dearth of 1595 that at Hertford, between 23 August and 8 November, the best wheat had risen in price by 14 per cent, 'second' quality wheat by 25 per cent, and 'third' by 27 per cent.[11]

In attempting to trace the course of dearth, then, we cannot examine quantities through prices; we must rely on prices alone. But the problem of *which* prices remains. The most extensive series available to us are of wheat prices, and the most frequently cited examples derive from Lord Beveridge's 'English average'. The deficiencies of this series are well known: they are principally institutional purchasing prices, behaving perhaps more like wholesale than retail prices; they derive from Southern England, neglecting those more northerly regions in which increasing numbers of people dwelt; and they are, of course, the prices of wheat, and not those cheaper grains and mixtures – barley, oats, and 'maslin' – that supplied the bread wants of so many consumers.

This last problem is usually countered by making wheat a proxy for other grains. When wheat rose sharply in price, it is argued, so also did the lesser grains. Thus Hoskins argues this for the first half of our period, using the price behaviour of wheat, oats and pulses in Lincoln market as a corroborative example. Hoskins went on to classify individual 'harvest years' (that is, the twelve months running from 29 September in one year to 28 September in the next) as experiencing harvests in one of six categories. These ranged from 'abundant', through 'good', to 'average', 'deficient', 'bad' and finally 'dearth' years, with the categories being defined by the degree to which the Beveridge average wheat price in an individual year deviated below or above a trend determined by a 31-year moving average. Thus the wheat harvest of 1550/1 was a 'bad' one, as was that of 1551/2, but these were succeeded by 'good' harvests in the following two years. By implication the yields of other grains might be similarly classified. Hoskins extended this classification of English harvests through to the harvest year 1759/60 (Hoskins, 1964 and 1968).

Not all were happy with these procedures. One historian was led to produce similar calculations using alternative sets of prices for the period 1465 to 1634 (Harrison, 1971). Using Bowden's price series for wheat, oats, and an average for 'all grains', he found many discrepancies in classifications and concluded that Hoskins

[11] *Calendar of State Papers Domestic, Elizabeth I, 1595–97*, p. 126.

'was wrong . . . to assume that wheat prices reflected other grain prices, let alone other food prices in general'. In 47 per cent of all cases their classification of wheat harvests varied by category; in 48 per cent of all cases there were discrepancies in classification between the Hoskins wheat series and the Bowden 'all grains' one. Most of these differences, however, involved a difference of only one category up or down, and we should remember that it requires only a small percentage difference to move the classification from one to another. Thus a rise of 29 per cent above trend puts the wheat harvest of 1594/5 into the 'bad' category for Hoskins, but a rise of 24 per cent puts the same year into the 'deficient' category for Harrison. A second, and more serious, charge, levelled by Appleby, is that all Harrison's calculations are incorrect since a computing error made the moving average for any particular year too high by 3 to 4 per cent (Appleby, 1975).

Appleby (1979) went on to offer a more potent objection to the use of a wheat price series as a general indicator of harvest qualities. He argued that there was a tendency in England for the prices of the lesser grains to move symmetrically with wheat down to about the year 1660, and for them to move independently – asymmetrically – from that time onwards. This general tendency, to which important demographic consequences were ascribed, was put down to increasing acreages of spring-sown crops (oats and barley) being grown at the expense of winter-sown wheat and rye. 'This diversification in grain crops', Appleby argued, 'provided a degree of protection against the weather which previously had been lacking'.

Where such developments occurred they could well have produced some protection, enabling farmers to increase their spring sowings when inclement weather inhibited the germination and growth of winter-sown crops. But, one potent generator of dearth – heavy and sustained rainfall through the summer and into the harvest periods – might be expected to continue to diminish yields, irrespective of when the crop was sown. An alternative explanation to that offered by Appleby might take in changes in the geography of grain cultivation, with increasing tendencies from the mid-seventeenth century for grain, especially barley, to be grown on light soils (Jones, 1965). Cold and wet weather would continue to hit wheat, especially that grown on heavy impermeable clays, but high precipitation would do less serious damage on those light soils in eastern England that cry out for water in so many years.

Appleby's explanation of what was happening may be questionable, but that some general changes in price relativities were taking place can perhaps be accepted. These, however, were general tendencies, not invariable rules. One can find years before 1660 when high wheat prices did not coincide with high barley prices (and vice versa), and occasional years after 1660 when symmetry is to be found. Wrigley has recently pointed to the coincidence of relatively cheap wheat and very expensive barley and oats in the harvest year 1600/1, and has argued that in 1608/9 a bad harvest in wheat coincided with cheap barley and only a moderate increase in the price of oats (1989, *255*). If asymmetry can be found before 1660, so also can symmetry be found afterwards. In fact an interesting example occurred almost immediately. The year 1661/2 was a dearth year for Hoskins, and it appears to have been accompanied by steep increases in the price of rye and lesser increases in the prices of oats and barley. Similarly the bad wheat harvests of 1673/4 and 1674/5 were matched, especially in the latter year, with quite sharply rising prices in the lesser grains and pulses. Appleby noted that the dearths of wheat in the 1690s were generally not accompanied by steeply rising barley and oats prices, and this appears to be true also of the dearth of 1708/9 and the bad harvest of 1709/10 (Appleby, 1979). But one should perhaps note that the bad wheat harvests of 1727/8 and 1728/9 appear to have been accompanied by the highest barley prices seen since the late 1640s (Bowden, 1985, *Appendix 1*).

'Severely bad harvests in which the wheat crop failed owing to harsh conditions at sowing time', Holderness has recently written, 'include 1756, 1766, 1768, 1789, 1795, 1800. . . . In many cases the spring was also backward and the barley crop light or sparse' (Holderness, 1985, *98*). At the very end of our period, in the harvest year 1800/1 the average price of wheat prevailing at Devizes market was over 157s per quarter. This can be compared with an average of 57s in the nine years 1790/1 to 1798/9. Barley prices rose to nearly 67s per quarter, compared to an average between 1790 and 1798 of 32s. Oats reached nearly 41s, compared to a previous average of less than 25s. At Devizes it would have been impossible for purchasers to have spent less in the dearth year of

Table 1 *High wheat price years (harvest years beginning Michaelmas);*
see text above

Period								
1550–99	1550,	**1551**	1555,	1556,	1560,	**1562,**	1565,	1573,
	1586,	1594,	1595,	1596,	1597			
1600–49	**1608,**	1613,	1622,	1630,	1647,	**1648,**	1649	
1650–99	1658,	**1661**	1673,	1674,	1678,	1692,	**1693,**	1695,
	1696,	**1697,**	**1698**					
1700–49	1708,	**1709,**	1713,	1727,	**1728,**	1739,	**1740**	
1750–99	**1756,**	1766,	1767,	1772,	1774,	1795,	**1799**	

Source: Beveridge Price Collection, London School of Economics, Box J 35.

1800/1 by trading down to the lesser grains (John, 1989, *Appendix 1*; see also Wells, 1988, *50–2*).

There is perhaps enough encouragement here to continue the belief that wheat price movements can be employed as rough markers for those years in which dearth was likely to have presented problems. Table 1 lists by half centuries those harvest years in which the Beveridge English annual average wheat price rose 20 per cent (and in bold type 35 per cent) above the trend established by a 31-year moving average. Such percentage rises are perhaps modest by the standards that prevailed in some other European countries, but they do serve to pick out, as we shall see, the principal years in which food prices gave rise to public concern in England.

The second half of the sixteenth century witnessed numerous years in which annual average prices rose by 20 per cent or more above trend: 26 per cent of all years experienced such leaps. Some respite came in the next 50 years as the frequency rate fell to 14 per cent, only for it to rise again to 22 per cent in the period 1650–99. Most of this increase, however, was concentrated in the 1690s, a decade of war as well as successively poor wheat harvests. The eighteenth century witnessed a return to early seventeenth-century frequencies, both halves of the century witnessing identical rates of 14 per cent. Dearths of this magnitude never disappeared in our period, therefore, though there was a noticeable decline in the frequency of the more severe events, as expressed by leaps of 35 per cent or more above trend. Here the most interesting development was the general decline that took place after the first half-century, with such leaps virtually disappearing in the second half of the eighteenth century. The crises of 1756 and 1799 are a reminder, however, that this scourge was never totally eliminated, and worse was to follow in 1800 and in a succession of years to 1816.

Before leaving this discussion of prices, two further considerations should be noted. One is that consumers might become alarmed about sudden leaps in prices in years when the average price turned out to be somewhat less than alarming (Outhwaite, 1981, *403–4*). A second is that in years when shortages were both real and prolonged, one often finds complaints that dealers were reluctant to sell in the small quantities, of bushels and half bushels, that those with small incomes could only afford to purchase (Thompson, 1971, *101–2*).

This supplies a reminder that dearth affected incomes as well as prices. A depleted harvest generated less work, and thus lower incomes, amongst agricultural labourers. It might also affect the processing industries that used grain as a raw material, cutting back activity and incomes there. Declining employment, coinciding with high food prices, might decrease demands for the cheaper consumer goods – clothing, footwear, and household articles. Labourers and artisans might, therefore, be doubly hit (Ashton, 1959). Indeed even moderately poor harvests might produce cries and signs of distress in manufacturing regions if such harvests coincided with independent economic dislocation and unemployment.

Defined as sudden leaps in grain prices, therefore, dearth had a continuing presence throughout this long period, and even moderate escalations in the cost of grain products might produce howls of protest from those whose incomes were insufficient, or from those whose livelihoods had been taken away. The intense complaints that came from wool growing and cloth manufacturing areas in the early 1620s owed as much to the collapse of their markets as to the high price of corn. The problem in Lincolnshire was said to be 'more of money than corn'. Even so, it was accompanied by a graphic picture of famine (Thirsk and Cooper, 1972, *24–5*). But how well grounded were such complaints? Did people starve and die, as contemporaries sometimes attested?

2
Crises of subsistence?

Introduction

'Did the peasants really starve?' This is the title of one chapter in Peter Laslett's *The World We Have Lost*, first published in 1965. The question was prompted by the work of continental scholars, such as Meuvret and Goubert, who had identified so-called 'crises of subsistence' periodically decimating the populations of certain parts of early modern northern Europe. These crises, it was argued, were marked by a conjunction of events: prices at dearth levels were accompanied by sudden and sharp increases in mortality, by decreases in nuptiality, and by contemporaneous falls in 'conceptions' (that is, baptisms traced back by nine months).

Back in 1965, Laslett could write that England in the seventeenth century 'was already immune from these periodical disasters'. 'Nearly all of the English registers which have been studied so far', he continued, 'yield entirely negative conclusions: they contain no examples of harvest years where a conspicuous rise in burials was accompanied by a corresponding fall in conceptions and in marriages'. An exception had to be made for the Cumberland parish of Greystoke, where an annotated register revealed several cases in 1623 where death was attributed to starvation, and an 'incomplete crisis of subsistence' may have been experienced in Ashton-under-Lyne, in Lancashire, in the same year (Laslett, 1965, *107–27*).

By 1983, and the third edition of *The World We Have Lost*, Laslett was less certain. He recognised that the 'theory of the *crise de subsistance*' had come under fire from French historians; that England may have been freer of such events than France or even

Scotland; but that conjunctions of high prices, with rising deaths, falling marriages and conceptions certainly existed. The year 1623 was now seen to have witnessed a widespread disaster through much of the highland zone of England, and altogether the 1983 edition conveyed more uncertainty in answering the question 'Did the peasants really starve?'

Since 1965 historians have revealed many of the complexities that subsistence crises present. In a world such as that of sixteenth- and early seventeenth-century England, where dearth was a persistent phenomenon and where 'crisis mortality' – sudden leaps in burials – were also common experiences in many communities, it was perhaps to be expected that high food prices and high mortality might occasionally coincide. Conjunctions might, therefore, be accidental rather than functional occurrences. Also, even if such occurrences were too frequent to be wholly accidental, the near simultaneous rise of food prices and of burials need not signify that people were dying of starvation or 'famine related mortality'. For example, some weather conditions that were likely to induce harvest failures – long sustained and bitter cold spells through the winter and spring – might also be propitious conditions for the dissemination of those diseases that tended to hit the poor and elderly. 'Abnormally low temperatures and cold, dense atmospheres', it has been pointed out, 'can result in deaths from the process of hypothermia, almost certainly facilitate the spread of respiratory infections, and probably lead to changes in the number of deaths from heart attacks and strokes' (Post, 1985, *51*). Long, bitter winters could also seriously disrupt economic activity, lowering earning capabilities as well as leading to increases in the cost of fuels. The poverty that accompanied high grain prices at the lowest levels of society, or the collapse of local economies, might induce higher rates of internal migration. With the poor wandering to new locations in search of relief or employment, communities were exposed to new diseases or fresh strains of old ones. Indeed, it has been argued that 'the rising incidence of infectious disease derived more from social disarray and dysfunctional behaviour than from dangerously lowered human resistance to pathogenic organisms' (Post, 1985, cited in the stimulating review of these problems in Walter and Schofield, 1989, *1–73*).

Even if dearth meant that many people witnessed a serious

deterioration in their nutritional status, this might not automatically lead to contemporaneous mortality peaks. Much would depend on what pathogens were currently circulating in the local environment, and the extent to which the population had previously been exposed to these disease agents. Even if previous exposure had been minimal, we must accept that not all diseases were major killers, and that some pathogens appear to have been relatively insensitive to the nutritional state of the host. Indeed, medical specialists have noted that 'in some special circumstances . . . malnutrition is more likely to discourage multiplication of the agent than to affect the resistance mechanisms of the host' (Scrimshaw, 1968, *16*). It must also be noted that even with diseases where this was not the case, the effects of malnutrition on mortality might not be immediately visible, since some afflictions, such as tuberculosis, have comparatively lengthy intervals between onset and fatal termination. Much depended, therefore, on what diseases were currently circulating. Here a major problem confronts the historian since it is frequently difficult to identify precisely just what it was that was ravaging our ancestors. Take, for example, the difficulties one encounters in understanding the causes of death in the London 'bills of mortality' (Landers and Mouzas, 1988). What exactly were 'convulsions', 'dropsy', 'spleen', 'fever', or, to take an extreme example, 'tympany'? The latter is thought to have been 'an excessive accumulation of abdominal gas or air' (Forbes, 1979, *130*). Most of these descriptions obviously relate more to symptoms than they do to causes, and we may wonder particularly what it was that induced the fatal fart.

Despite all these admissions of uncertainty, however, it would not be surprising to find in sixteenth- and early seventeenth-century England, some positive connections between dearth and death. Through much of this period population numbers were rising, and at times rising quite rapidly. It is arguable that, for long periods, population growth rates exceeded the rate at which agricultural productivity rose. The rise in population coincided with structural changes: increasing numbers of labourers and semi-skilled artisans; perhaps also rising numbers of small farmers, especially in the pastoral regions; increasing densities of population, again particularly in the pastoral regions; and increasing urbanisation. Decreasing proportions of the population were able to provide food for themselves; increasing proportions became dependent on the market for grain. A long-term problem here was the rise in grain prices that tended, perhaps almost everywhere, to outstrip increases in nominal wage rates. Increasing numbers were thus becoming harvest-sensitive, with this sensitivity becoming rawly exposed when, as periodically happened, the harvests failed (Wrigley and Schofield, 1981, *312–13*; Outhwaite, 1986; and, for warnings about the dangers of exaggerating these developments, Walter, 1989).

We should note also that, despite the medical and other reservations entered earlier, severe nutritional deficiency does appear to render the host more susceptible to many disease pathogens. The most comprehensive study that we have of the interactions between nutritional status and disease – the World Health Organization Report of 1968 – states, quite uncategorically, that 'nutritional deficiencies generally reduce the capacity of the host to resist the consequences of infection. An aggravation of disease, or synergism, is the expected result in man whenever nutritional deficiency is sufficiently severe' (Scrimshaw, 1968, *13*).

A conference on this subject, held at Bellagio in 1982, spent much time discussing the exceptions to these general rules, and exploring the complexities of possible linkages, but it could still conclude that 'nutritional deficiencies are capable of reducing resistance to infection and thereby increasing the prevalence and severity of many infections through a variety of [physiological] mechanisms' (Rotberg and Rabb, 1985, *307*; cf. Walter and Schofield, 1989, *17–21*). The relationship is not simply a one-way one – running from malnutrition to decreased resistance – since the onset of some diseases might themselves precipitate clinical malnutrition. 'Infectious disease', the 1968 WHO Report tells us, 'nearly always makes co-existing malnutrition worse', a view with which many at the Bellagio conference concurred (Rotberg and Rabb, 1985, *305*).

Economic and social historians could point to other reverse linkages between disease and deprivation. At the family level the death of a bread-winner might precipitate acute family poverty, and at a wider social level epidemics frequently produced severe economic disruption as trade and industry collapsed. Crises, whether produced by disease, dearth or trade collapses often induced migratory flows; these might relieve pressures at the epicentre of the crisis whilst increasing them at the periphery.

The interconnections then become even more complex. Migrants may have disseminated diseases, and with cold and poverty leading to the poor huddling indoors (in their homes, or in workhouses, jails or hospitals) for lengthy periods, propitious conditions were supplied for crowd diseases to exert their deadly consequences. One recent examination of the European-wide dearth of 1740–42 concluded that the 'connecting link between the subsistence crises and epidemic mortality proved to be more social than physiological' (Post, 1985, *28*).

What then have historians established? Until recently there existed a variety of studies of the relationships between grain prices and burials in particular communities and regions. The works of Appleby (1978), Chambers (1972), Clarkson (1975), Drake (1962), and Laslett (1965/83), yielded a bewildering variety of general opinions, if only because these scholars were using a variety of methodologies and were studying different regions and different periods. What was needed was a study of what might be happening over a long period, in a wide geographical area, and using a consistent methodology. This need was fulfilled by Wrigley and Schofield's monumental work, *The Population History of England, 1541–1871* (1981). It is, however, a work from which students can derive conflicting and misleading conclusions, and it has consequently to be mined with care.

'The most important factor in determining the level of the standard of living in the short run was the price of food', say Wrigley and Schofield (1981, ch. 8). Real wages (as determined by the Phelps Brown and Hopkins index) in harvest years beginning on 1 October are compared with burials in years beginning on 1 July. (The rationale for this is to be found in their observation that 'there is evidence to suggest that prices in the summer months began to reflect expectations about the harvest to be gathered in the autumn'; Wrigley and Schofield, 1981, *312*). This leads on to their 'top-twenty' analysis. Here they pick out the 20 years in each of four series (real wages, the crude death rate, the crude marriage rate, and the crude birth rate) when rates rose and fell most above and below the trend in each series (as established by 25-year moving averages). The relationships that are most relevant to us are what happened in the 20 years of most extreme deprivation (the years when food prices rose most above trend). These years were selected from the whole long period 1541 to 1871. Thus the most severe fall in real wages occurred in the harvest year 1596/7, the second most severe was in 1556/7, the third in 1710/11, and the fourth in 1800/1. How far, Wrigley and Schofield ask, do these top-twenty years of deprivation coincide with above average movements in mortality, and below average movements in nuptiality and fertility? The exercise revealed very positive relationships with both marriage and birth rates: in eighteen out of the twenty most deprived years these nuptiality and fertility measures fell below trend. The results on the mortality side, however, were altogether more mixed in that death rates were sometimes, but by no means always, above trend. In some years, such as 1555/6, 1649/50, and 1799/1800, the death rate was actually below average. Indeed, ten years in which the death rate was above average were neatly counterbalanced by ten in which deaths were below trend. (When the exercise was reversed, and the twenty most mortal years came under scrutiny, similar results were obtained. In the authors' words: 'very high death rates were not significantly associated with above-average food prices').

The top-twenty analysis of dearth-death relationships in chapter 8, however, needs to be handled carefully. We should remember that Wrigley and Schofield are here examining what was happening over the whole long period from 1541 to 1871, and not what was happening in particular, perhaps quite crucial, sub-periods. Nor were they examining behaviour in particular regions, and not all areas were equally disaster-prone. Thirdly, we should remember that the observation cited above, arguing that the worst episodes of crisis mortality were 'not significantly associated with above-average food prices' is largely irrelevant. No one denies that crisis mortality episodes frequently occurred in years of relative food abundance. It is what happens to mortality levels in, and after, periods of high prices that is our concern.

When the exercises were extended to take in events in the year immediately following those primarily under scrutiny, rather different observations were made:

The most definite conclusions to emerge . . . are therefore that extreme downward fluctuations in real wages were accompanied by marriage rates below trend in the same year and by birth rates below trend both in the same year and the following year. Extreme fluctuations in real wages had no effect on death rates in the current year, but there is reasonable evidence of connexion between very low real wages and higher than average death rates in the following year. Thus in England in the past the classic *crise de subsistance*, insofar as it was captured by the real-wage series, affected nuptiality and fertility much more than mortality (*328*).

These ideas are extended in the complex analysis, conducted by Ronald Lee in chapter 9 of *The Population History of England, 1541–1871*, of the interrelationships between wheat prices (not real wages) and ensuing annual series of births, marriages and deaths. What Lee found, using data for the period 1548 to 1834, was a positive statistical association between wheat prices and mortality, but a weak one. Sixteen per cent of all the short-run variation in mortality was positively associated with price changes. Most of these positive consequences occurred, however, not in the concurrent year but in the two succeeding ones. Only when prices rose to exceptional heights, such as in dearth years, did mortality rise in concurrent years. Lee went on to argue that the effect of wheat price movements on marriage variability was more pronounced (at 41 per cent), with the sharpest falls being experienced in the concurrent year, and that there was an even greater association with fertility (at 64 per cent).

We again need to remember that these are correlations established over a long period of time. But Lee also looked at relationships in particular sub-periods. In the first of these, the years 1548–1640, the correlation between prices and mortality rose to 22 per cent; in the second, the period 1641–1745, it fell to 17 per cent; and in the third, the years 1746–1834, it fell further to 15 per cent. The other correlations – of marriages and baptisms with prices – showed much less change over time (Wrigley and Schofield, 1981, *375*). These findings led Schofield to state of the period before 1640:

There was, therefore, a time when mortality in England fluctuated in sympathy with the harvest, but after 1640 this dependence was greatly attenuated, and by the mid-eighteenth century fluctuations in scarcity and plenty no longer found any echo in movements in the death rate (Schofield, in Rotberg and Rabb, 1985, *88*).

Such findings and statements have not gone unquestioned.

Galloway, using a different periodisation and correlating wheat prices with non-infant deaths, has argued that the period 1675 to 1755 saw a closer positive association of mortality and price fluctuations than the two long periods that preceded and followed these years. Much appears to depend on the placement of the overlapping period 1641–74, when mortality revealed a strongly negative response to prices (Galloway, 1988).

The geography and chronology of subsistence crises

The evidence presented so far suggests that deaths were once sensitive to price fluctuations, but it fails to answer questions about where this sensitivity was most powerfully felt, and about when and where it disappeared. To answer questions such as these we need to take note of the work of others, particularly those who have studied vital events in particular regions and localities.

There is some reason to believe that towns, with their access to greater communal wealth and with their superior relief organization, were relatively immune to these subsistence crises (Slack, 1979, *36*). Towns might be hit more frequently by severe mortality crises, but these events were less often dearth-related ones. Not that towns were totally immune: the worst famines, such as those of the 1590s, hit small market towns in abundance and even penetrated the poorer parishes of the metropolis (Appleby, 1978, *137–9*). We should note also that Galloway, correlating adult deaths in London with grain prices in the period 1670 to 1830, has argued recently that 'An increase in prices is clearly associated in deaths among Londoners in the middle and older age groups' (Galloway, 1985, *500*).

Despite the fact that rural dwellers may have been less exposed to the force of market economies (Walter, 1989), dearth was more of a problem in rural than in urban communities. But not all country districts suffered: some regions appear to have been particularly vulnerable, perhaps none more so than parts of the highland zone, and particularly those in the extreme north-west of England. Appleby demonstrated vividly the severity of the mortality leaps in many Cumberland and Westmorland parishes following the dearths of 1586/7, 1597/8 and 1623/4 (Appleby, 1978, *95*).

Appleby also clearly revealed why it was that the north-west was so vulnerable. The region was largely pastoral: grain growing was always risky and deficiencies were thus always likely to occur. The situation became more serious as population growth in the region created more marginal farms and more consumers. This happened in an era when the terms of trade were moving against pastoral products, thus lessening the region's purchasing power. He argued also that the position of many farmers was worsened by their having to pay high rents. Thus, for many reasons, the region was hit hard from the late sixteenth century by acute harvest failures, and the situation was compounded in the early seventeenth century by weaknesses and depression in the wool and textile markets. He was led to argue that 'there were two Englands, one subject to trade depressions and harvest failure but able to avoid widespread starvation, the other pushed past the edge of subsistence by these same dislocations' (Appleby, 1973, *430*).

The Cambridge Group subsequently adopted this idea of two Englands, a division especially evident in the crises of 1586/8, 1596/8 and 1622/3. Wrigley and Schofield state that:

Before the mid seventeenth century there would therefore seem to be two Englands: one pastoral and remote, and the other engaged in arable farming but with a high degree of occupational specialization reflected in a relatively dense network of small towns. While access to grain, together with ease of transport and the well-developed communications in the south-east made the area much less vulnerable to harvest failures, its greater economic integration facilitated the spread of disease (Wrigley and Schofield, 1981, *677–8*).

This division between a remote and vulnerable pastoral highland north-west and a more flourishing, lowland arable, and economically well-integrated south may overemphasise divisions in several respects. Geographically things were more complicated than this. Subsistence crises were likely to occur wherever there prevailed the sort of conditions that Appleby described. Such events were possible in upland areas or in poor soil lowland regions; in pastoral areas – wherever situated – that were dependent generally on grain imports; in districts where there were lots of small farmers, labourers and artisans; in communities struggling to cope with industrial change and depression; in parts of England where communications were perhaps difficult. It is difficult to be totally prescriptive about preconditions. Walter and Schofield warn that 'no single factor was fatal'. What made areas vulnerable was 'a combination of unfavourable factors' (Walter and Schofield, 1989, *22–5*).

All sorts of additional things might tip a local economy into disaster. There were complaints on the western coast in 1629 of hunger-starved Irish 'boat people' landing in the area.[1] War-time provisioning requirements might bleed an area of food; the mobilization of troops in port towns frequently strained local provisioning, particularly if the troops were held there by such things as unfavourable winds (Stevenson, 1974, *47*). Contrariwise, the demobilization of troops put strain on local economies on occasion. Ashton noted long ago that most of the dearths of the eighteenth century occurred in periods of war, making importation more costly and difficult (Ashton, 1959, *34*).

Areas might be altogether less vulnerable if they were lowland ones with good communications; if they were mixed-farming areas with arable predominance; or if they had non-agricultural activities not under simultaneous strain. Communities that had resident gentry and well organised parochial machinery, able to organise emergency supplies or poor relief, may also have coped better with these disasters (Walter and Schofield, 1989, *24–5*).

Appleby's views have clearly supplied an important framework of reference for much recent work on the geography of subsistence crises in early modern England. His views on the chronology of famine have perhaps been even more influential. In his initial investigation of the major dearths of the late sixteenth and early seventeenth centuries in Cumbria, Appleby argued that the subsistence crises of 1597 and 1623 were perhaps the last to scar this region. The bad harvest of 1630/1 left this region relatively unscathed (Appleby, 1973). Later, in his book *Famine in Tudor and Stuart England*, he reiterated these conclusions about events in Cumbria, whilst extending his observations geographically. He was now prepared to argue that the four years of dearth before 1598 'brought extreme hardship to most – perhaps all – of England. Famine stalked the north and some parts of the south in 1597'. It also 'ranged across the north in 1623, with its center in the northwestern counties of Cumberland and Westmorland and in

---

[1] *Acts of the Privy Council, 1628–29*, pp. 297, 419.

northern Lancashire'. From time to time thereafter grain prices soared (1630/1, 1647/9, 1661/2 and the 1690s were singled out) but their mortality repercussions were 'limited in both intensity and effect' (Appleby, 1978). It was for these reasons that Laslett was persuaded to argue that the 1620s saw the last widespread subsistence-mortality crisis in England (Laslett, 1983). Wrigley and Schofield also write that 'The vulnerability of the upland north-west to harvest failure disappeared after 1623' (Wrigley and Schofield, 1981, 679), a judgement echoed by Walter and Scho-field (1989, 22) who went on to argue that 'By the mid seventeenth century . . . England had slipped the shadow of famine' (36). There is, therefore, a strongly voiced view that the impact of dearth on mortality was greatly diminished by the middle of the seventeenth century, and perhaps even before this.

Causes of the decline in harvest sensitivity

The decline of the vulnerability of the extreme north-west, Appleby thought, depended on the interaction of several forces. In the course of the seventeenth century the population of the region shrank, and the shrinkage was most marked in those upland communities that had proved so vulnerable at times of crisis. Coastal parishes, and inland towns such as Penrith and Kendall, showed more demographic buoyancy. There were declines also in the number of small, economically marginal tenants, and increases in the proportions of those employed in trade and industry. The region was helped as prices moved in favour of animals and animal products, and away from grain, and as activities such as coal and lead mining, iron production, and the knitting of stockings ex-panded and integrated the region much more fully into the national economy (Appleby, 1978). Many of these tendencies were also at work outside the north-west and thus they may have a wider applicability. Later, Appleby was to add his ingenious suggestion that it was the growth after about 1660 of an asymmetrical relation-ship between wheat and barley prices, consequent upon a changing balance of spring-sown as against winter-sown grain crops, that lay behind England's growing immunity to subsistence crises (see above, p. 10 and Appleby, 1979).

Historians have since compiled a long list of developments thought to have had such immunizing effects. Pride of place should perhaps go to the change in the rate of growth of population. Growth slowly subsided in the first half of the seventeenth century and this was followed by a population decline and slow recovery for the next one hundred years. A century of relative population stagnation after 1640 eased demands for grains, and encouraged those diversifying developments in agriculture that helped to raise arable yields. If farmers continued to absorb the same amount of grain for seed, animal use, and their own consumption, then net yields should have risen. In these circumstances, as Wrigley has demonstrated, marketable quantities would fluctuate much less than in the past (Wrigley, 1989).[2] 'Improvements in transportation and better market integration', it has also been suggested, 'made it easier to iron out regional deficiencies' (Walter and Schofield, 1989, *42*; Walter, 1989, *80–1*). Whilst it is hard to deny the force of such arguments, it is perhaps easy to overrate their significance. After all, the number of grain consumers also rose, and the volatility of the price of wheat, the most marketable of the grains, fell only slightly before the mid-eighteenth century (Galloway, 1988, *281*). This suggests that as much attention should be paid to income shifts as to supply changes.

Changes in the population curve affected both the supply of labour and the prices of basic foodstuffs, leading to some improvement in levels of real wages after the middle of the seventeenth century. Fuller employment and shifts in the occupational structure of the working population (away from agriculture and towards trade and industry) may also have raised income per worker. Per capita expenditures on food generally may not have fallen (Shammas, 1983), for consumers might take the opportunity to 'trade up' to more expensive foodstuffs. This would, however, leave room for some 'trading down' in periods of dearth. Family expenditures should also have been relieved by the fall in average

---

[2] This can be illustrated by assuming a notional and constant deduction of 3 bushels per acre for seed and feed requirements. A 25 per cent deficiency on gross yields when yields averaged 6 bushels an acre would mean that only 1.5 bushels would be available for the market. But a 25 per cent shortfall when gross yields averaged 12 bushels an acre would mean that 6 bushels could be marketed. Thus a doubling of gross yields might lead to a fourfold increase in the amount marketed, despite an identical percentage harvest shortfall.

family size that must have ensued from the combination of high infant and child mortality and comparatively low levels of fertility that marked the post-1640 period. Improvements in wealth could lead to the acquisition of a few modest possessions – clothes or household goods – articles that might be pawned or sold to allow their owners to survive hard times. Fuller and wider implementation of the Elizabethan poor law, provoked perhaps by the crisis of the 1590s, sheltered the respectable helpless poor, some of whom had figured prominently as victims in crises in the past (Slack, 1988, *48–55, 170–82*; Walter and Schofield, 1989, *69, 81–3*). It may also have helped to reduce the extent of itinerant vagrancy (Post, 1985, *183*).

One can produce lengthy catalogues of developments that may have relieved populations of the deadlier consequences of dearth. It is much more difficult, however, to attach weights to these possible causes of improvement. Some doubts must remain also about the degree to which England had achieved immunity by the middle of the seventeenth century. Historians of dearth in Europe, as distinct from England, are inclined to place the turning-point a hundred years later around 1750 (Flinn, 1974; Post, 1985), and there are some grounds for thinking that this might apply to England also (see above pp. 20–1, and chapter 5 below).

3
Public policy

Serious harvest failures occurred throughout this long period 1550–1800, though with varying frequency, and it is clear that they were often accompanied by economic disruption and by hardship that was sufficiently pronounced to have marked demographic consequences. Men and women put off marriage, births fell, some unfortunates died, whilst some others took to the road in search of work or relief. Whether at home or in some new locality, men and women sought relief from the calamity or periodic dearth in various ways: through the adoption of modes of behaviour that reduced the risks of hardship and penury – what might be called life-insurance strategies (Outhwaite, 1985); through individual and collective acts of charity (Walter, 1989); and through the remedies pressed on communities by those in positions of political authority. It is the latter – responses of government to dearth – that supply the subject matter of this chapter. These public policy measures can be divided into three categories, though in truth there was considerable overlap between them. They are: (1) the controls exercised over the overseas trade in grains; (2) issues of the 'Book of Orders' for the relief of dearth; and (3) the supplementary controls imposed on alternative uses for grains.

Controls on the overseas grain trade

Parliamentary statutes had long curbed the free export of corn and many other victuals. These Corn Acts laid down certain floor prices for grains, above which exportation was prohibited, and below which it was permitted. These floor prices were periodically revised upwards, such as in 1555, 1563, 1593, 1604, 1624, 1656, and 1663. The floor price for wheat in 1555 stood at 6s 8d per quarter; by 1663 it had risen to 48s per quarter. These upward revisions occurred in a period of food price inflation. If the old floor prices had continued without revision, then exportation would never have been permitted. Revisions came generally in response to pleas from corn-growing districts, in years of abundance, that some exportation should be allowed. The revisions were, however, conservative ones. The general effect of these statutes was to curb exports. The latter could only occur legally in good harvest years, when prices occasionally fell below the floor prices, or by an exporter obtaining a royal licence to evade the statutes.

In 1670, however, a statute was passed totally freeing corn exports of the old price restraints. Grain could now be exported irrespective of the level of domestic prices, though some low customs duties had to be paid on these exports. These duties were subsequently removed in the Act of 1689. In the Corn Act of 1663, moreover, heavy duties were for the first time imposed on imported corn when prices in England were below certain specified levels, and in 1670 a graduated sliding scale of duties on corn imports was introduced. Just to confirm these radical changes in policy, in 1672 a bounty on exports was introduced as a temporary encouragement, and this was made permanent in 1689. Thereafter there were no radical changes in policy until, in 1773, price restraints were once more placed on corn exports: wheat, for example, could only be exported when its price was below 44s per quarter (Barnes, 1930; Gras, 1915; Outhwaite, 1981).

The background to all this is, of course, that rising trend of grain prices to about 1650, a succeeding phase of falling and static prices to about 1750, and renewed pressure on domestic grain supplies thereafter.

In periods of dearth further measures might be taken to control the overseas grain trade. It was common in the second half of the sixteenth century and the first half of the seventeenth century for governments to suspend exports, usually via a royal proclamation to this effect. It might be wondered why this was done, since the statutes made exporting illegal in such high-price years. A technical reason may have been to suspend exports by licence, but the measure also had a powerful advertising effect. It showed that government was taking the situation seriously.

These general suspensions occurred with some frequency in years of high prices down to 1632, and on several occasions in the later 1630s the Privy Council instructed customs officers in particular ports not to permit the export of grain. The dearth of the later 1640s saw the Council of State offering, though somewhat belatedly, similar instructions (Outhwaite, 1981; Thirsk, 1985, 305).

Thereafter, though bad harvests presented several opportunities for intervention, there were no such curbs imposed until the 1690s. In the dearth of 1693 a royal proclamation was issued attempting to prevent the export of corn to France. It is significant, however, that the old statutes against middlemen dealers of Edward VI's reign had now to be invoked. All the Corn Acts down to, and including, that of 1624 had given the Crown the right to suspend exports in times of dearth. This provision was omitted, perhaps not surprisingly, from the Protectorate Corn Act of 1656, and it is significant that it did not reappear in the Act of 1663, despite the restoration of the monarchy three years earlier. A further attempt was made by the Lords Justices in October 1698 to curb exports by invoking the Edwardian statutes against forestalling, regrating and engrossing. That this had limited success is indicated by the fact that it was eventually necessary for a somewhat reluctant parliament to suspend, by means of statute, grain exports for a year from February 1699, by which time the crisis was virtually over (Outhwaite, 1978).

This pattern of initially limited, and delayed effective, intervention continued into the eighteenth century. Although signs of disaster were evident in relation to wheat prices in 1708, and there was governmental anxiety about high prices and exports in the spring of 1709, the House of Commons was apparently reluctant to act.[1] It was not until a further bad harvest intervened that the executive in October 1709 again invoked the Edwardian middlemen statutes, and two further months lapsed before parliament passed an act to suspend exports.[2] The bad harvests of

---

[1] *Calendar of Treasury Books, 1709*, pp. 125, 167, 176, 369.
[2] R. R. Steele, *Tudor and Stuart Proclamations* (Oxford, 1910) I, 530; *Journal of the House of Lords*, XIX, 4, 18.

1727/8 and 1728/9 seem to have elicited little central government response.[3] Although we are told that 'unusually prompt action was taken in anticipation of a bad harvest in 1740' (Thirsk, 1985, *332*), we should remember that the harvest of 1739 was poor in certain regions and that prices were rising steeply by the mid summer of 1740 (Post, 1985, *119*). Once again all the government could do was to try to use, in late June 1740, the middlemen statutes of 5 and 6 Edward VI to hinder exportation, before parliament was persuaded to set in motion an export ban in late November. This enabled the government to act in anticipation of the statute, which did not receive the royal assent until late March.[4] Prices rose markedly again in 1756, as a result of the sustained rainfall of that year, but it was not until December, after several months of serious rioting, that a statute was passed banning the export of grain. This measure was re-enacted in 1757 and 1758, and the ban was complemented by additional measures such as that which discontinued the payment of duties on imported grain (Ashton, 1959, *21*; Barnes, 1930, *31–8*; Charlesworth, 1983, *88*).

The period from the mid-seventeenth to the mid-eighteenth century thus saw a pattern of initial attempts being made by ministers to halt exports of corn, usually by invoking the Edwardian statutes against middlemen, followed, often belatedly, by parliamentary statutes suspending exports. On occasions executives may have been forced into employing the Edwardian statutes by the fact that parliament was not then sitting, but ministers also had to be careful. The right of the Crown to suspend grain exports in periods of emergency had ended with the lapse of the statute of 1624. There were thus constitutional arguments inhibiting ministerial interference; they had to be careful not to breach the principle embodied in the Bill of Rights of 1689, namely 'That the pretended power of suspending of laws, or the execution of laws, by regal authority, without consent of parliament, is illegal'. There

---

[3]   Thirsk, 1985, *332*, seems to be alone in arguing that there was a general ban on exports in these years. There is no mention of such a ban in the Commons or Lords Journals, *Statutes at Large*, or in such secondary authorities as Barnes and Ashton.

[4]   *Calendar of Treasury Books, 1739–41*, pp. 252–3, 284; *Journal of the House of Lords*, XXV, pp. 544, 547, 639.

were also powerful landed and mercantile interests to overcome, many of them with a voice in parliament.

Many of these points can be illustrated by events in the dearth of 1766. The problems began at least a year earlier. In August 1765 acts permitting the import of duty-free grain and the suspension of export bounties both lapsed. This appears to have led in the months that followed to merchants exporting (and claiming bounties on) grain that they had previously imported duty free. This anomaly was rectified in January–February 1766 by reimposition (until 29 September) of the duty remissions and bounty suspensions by parliament, and it was accompanied by a ban on the export of grain and flour until 26 August 1766. Given what happened the previous summer it is surprising that parliament took no steps to extend the export embargo before it recessed in June 1766. Late frosts and a wet summer hit the harvest of 1766 badly, and crops also failed over large parts of Europe. By August there were reports that grain was rising rapidly in price and moving towards the ports for export. Pleas were made by a number of towns for a reimposition of the export ban, and the government, under Chatham, after first proclaiming the Edwardian middlemen statutes on 10 September, issued on 26 September an Order in Council imposing a further embargo on grain exports. This gave rise to a vigorous parliamentary debate about the constitutional legality of such action, and although it overrode the ensuing opposition, the government felt it necessary to pass an act indemnifying customs officers responsible for enforcing the embargo (Barnes, 1930, *38–40*; Lawson, 1986; Shelton, 1973, *25–46*). A similar situation arose in 1789 (Barnes, 1930, *53*).

The pressure on agriculture deriving from expanding populations, especially in the now burgeoning towns, and from the growth of industries was by the 1760s leading to a change in the balance of exports and imports of grainstuffs. One sign of this was that 'the liberty to export corn, as well as the payment of a bounty, was almost continuously suspended from 1765 to 1774' (Perren, 1989, *210*), and from 1 January 1774 statutory price restraints on exports were once more imposed by the act of 1773 (Barnes, 1930, *40–5*).

Books of orders

The origins of the 'Book of Orders for the Relief of Dearth', first issued by the Privy Council to counteract the dearth of 1586/7, appear to derive from the commissions issued in 1527 to deal with the calamitous failure of that year. It was then that the principal weapon appears to have been forged. Commissioners were appointed to survey particular districts, establishing what stores of grain existed in each locality, and to bind those with surpluses to bring supplies to their local markets. These commissioners were also urged to regulate the activities of middlemen (Heinze, 1976, *99–103*). Similar measures were instituted in the deficient years of 1549/50 and 1550/1, and again in the dearth of 1556/7 (Slack, 1980b). In 1586/7, however, these directions were codified into the printed *Orders devised by the especiall commandement of the Queenes Maiestie, for the reliefe and stay of the present dearth of Graine within the Realme.*[5] These *Orders*, with occasional modifications and additions, reappeared in 1594, 1595, 1608, 1622, and for what proved to be the last time, in 1630. Although there were pleas for a reissue in 1662, and the *Orders* were reprinted, they were never circulated. Over a hundred years later, in 1758, the *Orders* were privately reprinted and urged upon government officials, but once again the book was never officially issued (Slack, 1980a).

It is difficult to provide a concise summary of the contents of these books. That of 1595 comprised nearly 60 paragraphs of detailed instruction and exhortation running over 22 printed pages. Rigorous searches were to be made for stocks of grain that were surplus to the holder's domestic requirements. The justices were then to order those with such stocks to bring every week to named places in the locality specified quantities, there to be sold in open market to ordinary consumers in small measures or to licensed dealers. The latter were to be strictly regulated and watched, as also were the numbers, credentials, and activities of such as maltsters, brewers, alehouse-keepers, bakers and millers. The poor were to be looked after in various ways: they were to be given rights of pre-

---

[5] Extensive extracts from a draft version of the 1587 *Orders* are printed in E. M. Leonard, *The Early History of English Poor Relief* (Cambridge, 1900), pp. 318–26, and a summary of the entire contents of the 1587 set is in Gras, 1915, pp. 236–40.

emption in the markets; rich farmers were exhorted to sell to them at 'charitable prices' (either in the markets or to the local poor at the farm gate); the unemployed were to be set to work, and vagabonds punished. Alternative uses for bread grains were to be curbed. Much was demanded of the JPs. Not only were they to organise the searches and the supply of markets, they were also to watch over virtually all transactions, search out and punish offenders, and report monthly in writing on prices in their local markets and on 'their doings and proceedings by force of these instructions'.

These sprawling sets of good intentions were imposed by the Privy Council with some enthusiasm in successive crises from that of 1586/7 onwards, with this system of intervention reaching its apogee in the dearth of the harvest year 1630/1. Why then were the *Orders* never issued officially in any of the later harvest crises? One answer to this is largely political. The *Orders* were an exercise of the royal prerogative, and the multiplication of such exercises in the period of personal rule in the 1630s eventually produced a reaction to such executive actions. Charles I's government may also have made a mistake in continuing to press for their operation throughout 1631 and 1632, when events probably did not merit such rigorous interventionary policies. There is no doubt that this produced disenchantment, even resentment. What we must also remember is that these dearth measures were extraordinarily involved and bureaucratically time-consuming. The EEC commissioners at Brussels would have been proud of them. Heavy burdens were thrust upon the JPs. Any slackening on their part was supposed to be reported, and indeed the Privy Council frequently found itself complaining about the slackness of the Justices. Local notables might be prepared to put up with this in a period of emergency, provided the emergency was real and the demands not frequently recurrent. In the longer run it was perhaps suspicion of executive, non-parliamentary, actions, increasing awareness of the clumsiness of the dearth orders, and growing appreciation of alternative methods of dealing with the problems that killed off issues of the *Book of Orders*. The poor, for example, could be relieved directly, in the localities where there really was a problem, by direct doles of money or supplies. This was thought to be preferable to imposing a strait-jacket on the whole internal and external grain trade (Outhwaite, 1981; Slack, 1980a).

Supplementary controls

The *Orders* themselves contained, as we briefly noted, curbs on alternative uses for food grains. Grain was not to be fed to dogs, or to other beasts; sheep should not be fed with peas and beans; starch-making was to be suspended; and crack-downs on drinking were urged. The latter usually took the form of attempts to regulate malting, the strength and price of beer, and the number of ale-houses and tippling houses.

Such measures were frequently supplemented with royal procla-mations and conciliar orders. These appear to have a similar history to those attempts to halt the export of corn: they are frequent down to the 1630s and virtually non-existent from the 1660s to the 1690s. In the eighteenth century some of these measures begin to make a reappearance. As we have seen, there were several attempts to suspend exports of corn via proclamation; starch-making was suspended in 1795 and in 1800; and the use of wheat and barley for distilling was restricted in 1757, 1767–8, 1773–4, 1782–4, 1788, and 1796–8 (Ashton, 1959; Barnes, 1930).

But not everything later reappeared: centrally-inspired govern-ment assaults on ale and beer drinking appear to have lapsed. One reason for this may lie with the development of more effective local controls over alehouses. Magistrates had now instituted stricter licensing of alehouses, even though by the eighteenth century they were no longer bothering to set the Assize of Ale. The absence of old-style suspensions of malting and suppressions of tippling houses owes something also to the growth of the excise – the 'golden goose of government revenue', as Clark has aptly termed it. Curtailment of beer and ale drinking diminished the revenue. 'The more Ale Houses there are the better it is for the Excise', revenue officials candidly admitted in 1685 (Clark, 1983, *179*; Mathias, 1959, *125–6*). Spirit distilling, subjected to a more sustained barrage of critical propaganda, however, was to succumb to periodic suspensions in the second half of the eighteenth century.

One can see, therefore, from the mid-1630s onwards a de-creasing tendency for central government – the Privy Council or parliament – to intervene in periods of dearth. Some types of centrally-inspired intervention returned in the eighteenth century, but involvement was generally belated and more limited in scope than the immediate and wholesale set of assaults on the problems that had characterised these emergencies in the earlier period. Thus from the mid-seventeenth century a vacuum was created in relation to control. This raises the question of whether this was simply filled by local officers, JPs and others, intervening under their own auspices, without prompting from the political centre. Did local government take over responsibility for managing these crises?

Local intervention

Even at the height of central government involvement, considerable time and effort had to be expended by the Privy Council in getting JPs and local commissioners to act. When the Council ceased to involve itself, these local officers were left to their own devices. Some continued to intervene in the old ways. In Wiltshire in 1647 the JPs insisted on public marketing, and prohibited sales by sample; they also curtailed the activities of the county's leading maltster. In Cheshire, controls were placed on corn badgers and on maltsters. Searches for stocks of grain were also carried out. Similar developments took place in Huntingdonshire and parts of Lancashire. The bad harvests of 1661/2, 1673/4 and 1674/5 saw more such activity in certain counties. 'These dearth years, and the more serious ones in 1696, 1697 and 1709', it has been argued, 'were survived on the basis of such local initiatives' (Fletcher, 1986, *199–200*). Thus there was some continuation of intervention at the local level. But we should remember that such activity was never universal, even at its height, and it probably became less widespread as the seventeenth century progressed.

There were good reasons why this should be so. One is that the dearth measures never were universally applicable; they always had more relevance to some areas than others (Fletcher, 1986, *193–9*). Their general application always required strong encouragement from the centre, and from the mid-seventeenth century this pressure was not forthcoming. Also, as time passed, methods of marketing changed. Historians have familiarised us with the trends: the decline of open marketing, and the rise of private bargaining, the growth of sale by sample, and of deals made by prior contract (Chartres, 1977; Everitt, 1967). As intervention became more piecemeal, its effectiveness decreased. Islands of intervention in seas that are uncontrolled are generally doomed. Market flows are simply distorted, as sellers shun the controlled in favour of the uncontrolled markets. JPs also began to put up persuasive arguments against intervention, pleading, for example, that it was likely to encourage hoarding and consumer panic (Slack, 1980a, *12*).

This is not to say that there was no local intervention by the eighteenth century. One can find plenty of examples of local initiatives, but, as with centrally-inspired interventionist policies, such measures were generally limited and belated. There were increasing tendencies for the authorities to *respond* to social disturbances in periods of dearth by invoking old policies rather than, as happened in earlier periods, for authority to implement such measures in order to *anticipate* such troubles.

4

Social disturbance

'Social disturbance', 'popular disorder', 'public violence', all these terms and more have been used by historians to describe those occasions when groups of men and women assembled and, according to authority, assisted each other in perpetrating offences against property or the person. The charges against people involved in such breaches of public order could be variously expressed – unlawful assembly, affray, or riot – and these offences were themselves variously defined in the past. In Common Law, for example, a riot was defined as an actual disturbance involving as few as three mutual perpetrators, but the Riot Act of 1715 made it an offence for a group of twelve or more to remain assembled after the Act had been proclaimed, irrespective of whether a violent disturbance had actually taken place. Some riots were classed as felonies, others as misdemeanours. Here again the law and its implementation varied through time (Stevenson, 1979, 5–11). The essential distinguishing feature was the contemporary perception of the ultimate intentions of the rioters, and thus the extent to which those in authority felt threatened by such activities. We should always remember that our view of these events is filtered through the eyes and actions of government (Manning, 1988, 56; Wells, 1978). It is largely those events that alarmed governing élites that come to our attention, and how we categorise them is to some considerable extent dependent on how they categorised them.

Problems of categorisation do beset us. Although this chapter intends to survey those collective disturbances that were noticed by authority in years of dearth, not all of these assemblies may have been riots, and not all of the disturbances may have been provoked by high food prices. Some assemblies may simply have been demonstrations; some may have had political roots and objectives; coincidence with dearth could be largely fortuitous. Election riots, religious disturbances, attacks on immigrants, all of these could occur in good years as well as bad ones. The intention, however, is to concentrate on those disturbances in which the immediate concerns of the participants were with the prices and availability of foodstuffs. Food or grain riots must be our staple fare.

The frequency of rioting

The counting of food riots is a perilous activity. 'No single major source is', we have been warned, '. . . without quite serious limitations' (Wells, 1978 and 1988). Although it has been argued, for example, that 'central government closely concerned itself with outbreaks of rioting in conditions of scarcity' (Walter and Wrightson, 1976, 26), reliance upon its records must meet the objection that riots were not always reported back to London, for fear of the consequences that might ensue. Local officials might be castigated for their deficiencies in allowing such disturbances to occur. Troops might be sent in to restore order, burdening the locality with extra mouths to feed, as well as creating local resentments that might linger for years afterwards. Combining several record sources to obtain a fuller picture is the obvious answer, but even this device runs into difficulties. Record sources are more abundant and generally contain fewer breaks as the historian moves forward in time. Thus it has been argued that 'one of the major difficulties . . . in determining the changing incidence of food or enclosure disturbances between 1500 and 1800 is the variation in the availability of newspaper sources' (Fletcher and Stevenson, 1985, 28). It must also be pointed out that no region has been subjected to this sort of lengthy intensive historical scrutiny. If one adds in the problems of defining and categorising riots, then the difficulties can be appreciated.

One recent study of the late sixteenth and early seventeenth centuries has stressed the comparative infrequency of 'dearth-related disorder' in this period. The records of central government, Walter and Wrightson note, render a total of only about 40 outbreaks of grain rioting in the years from 1585 to 1660: 'years of dearth', they emphasise, 'were not marked by widespread rioting' (1976, *26*). Several years later, however, Walter drew attention to over 70 incidents of food rioting in the period 1585–1649 (in Charlesworth, 1983, *72–80*). Despite this inflation of the number of incidents, he was still prepared to argue that 'Years of harvest failure in England in this period were not scarred by widespread food riots' (Walter, 1985, *47*). The increase may have owed something to more intensive research, and a tendency to report as separate incidents those that fulminated at short intervals in any one locality. It does not appear to be due, however, to Walter categorising as food riots, disturbances that might be classified in some other way. But here also we must recognise a problem. There is some potentiality for demarcation disputes amongst historians of riot.

Groups pressurised by deteriorations in their economic circumstances might express their frustrations in various ways: those in towns might attack the shipments or premises of grain dealers – the classic food riot; those in industrial areas might vent their frustrations on the workplaces of those employers who were no longer putting out work to them – 'Luddism' as it came to be called in a later period; and those in country parishes might throw down hedges – enclosure riots. Indeed, a great variety of angry responses have been encountered, running from the posting of anonymous libels, to arson and cattle maiming. A recent study of 'village revolts' has argued that 'anti-enclosure riots were a much more widespread form of protest in the sixteenth and early seventeenth centuries than grain riots'. The 125 cases produced for the Jacobean period alone perhaps bear this out (Manning, 1988, *23, 82*). Enclosure here takes in, however, not only the classic transformations of open-field into enclosed farming systems, and encroachments onto commons by improving landlords, but also the 'privatisation' by the Crown of royal forests and wetlands. Although Manning does not provide a detailed chronology of such anti-enclosure riots, he does see, in the Elizabethan period, a marked increase in such disturbances in the 1590s, an increase he is inclined to put down to population pressure rather than to harvest failure. In truth, whilst enclosures could occur at any time, outbreaks of resentment against them were often precipitated by dearth.

A good example is provided by the 'Western Rising' of 1626–32, a succession of disturbances centred on the royal forests in Dorset, Wiltshire and Gloucestershire that were provoked by the Crown's attempts to wring profit out of these assets by disposing of them to courtiers and speculators. Riots erupted in Gillingham, Dorset, in 1626, largely as a consequence of attempts which began the year before to disafforest the area, and they continued intermittently there to 1628. Here there was no background of dearth. At the same time, disafforestation of Braydon, Wiltshire, was being undertaken, but rioting here was delayed until mid 1631. This appears to have touched off events in nearby Chippenham Forest. Disafforestation began in Feckenham in November 1627, but again it was not until 1631 that rioting broke out. That year also witnessed eruptions in the Forest of Dean. Those principally affected by these developments were the squatters, cottagers who had no official commoning rights and whose livelihood was threatened by the attempts to parcel up existing commons for private use. How far, one wonders, were these outbreaks precipitated by the dearth of 1630/1, a dearth that raised food prices and reduced markets for the goods produced by these poor cottager artisans? Sharp has recently written, 'Over one half of the food riots for the entire period 1586–1631 occurred between 1629 and 1631 . . .'. These were undoubtedly years when there were considerable anxieties about the price of grain, though he is inclined to lay more causal responsibility at the door of unemployment in the textile industries in generating these disturbances (Sharp, 1980, *10–42, 82–125*).

For a variety of reasons, therefore, attempts to survey the history and geography of grain riots have to be accompanied with more than a pinch of scepticism. One careful exercise of this type has argued that the dearth of 1586/7 produced three or four known food riots; and that the succession of catastrophes between 1594 and 1598 produced only twelve. The bad harvest of 1608/9 produced perhaps two such incidents, that of 1613/14 four, and that of 1622/3 perhaps six. But 'A deadly combination of trade depression and harvest failure . . . brought a notable increase in disorder in the period 1629–31'; 30 food or grain riots have been counted for this period. The three bad harvest years running from 1647 to 1650 produced fourteen such events. The dearths of the

1690s saw increased social turbulence: 24 incidents are recorded for the years 1693–5 (Charlesworth, 1983, *72–80*).

It is, however, the eighteenth century that appears to have witnessed the most extraordinary rise in the extent and frequency of such behaviour. 'A number of nationwide waves of food rioting have been identified after 1700', writes Stevenson, 'such as those of 1709–10, 1727–9, 1739–40, 1756–7, 1766–8, 1772–3, 1783, 1795–6, 1799–1801, 1810–13, and 1816–18' (Stevenson, 1979, *91*). Rioting was widespread in 1740, when the deficient harvest of 1739 was followed by dearth in 1740. At least sixteen counties were affected by rioting in the latter year (Malcolmson, 1981, *113*). Over 140 incidents took place in at least 30 counties, however, in the dearth year of 1756/7, and over 24 counties were involved in the disturbances of 1766 (Charlesworth, 1983, *86*; Malcolmson, 1981, *113*). The events of this latter year have been described as 'the most extensive rural disorders in a century when food riots became chronic' (Shelton, 1973, *21*), but even these must pale into insignificance behind the extensive disorders precipitated by the bad harvests of 1795/6 and 1799/1800. Stevenson's estimate of 128 riots nationally in these years is acknowledged to be a serious underestimate, neglecting to notice many disturbances in the north-west of England (Booth, 1977; Stevenson, 1974, *35–7*). Bohstedt has advanced the total for the single year 1800 to one of over 200, and has argued that Devon alone witnessed 43 food riots in the aftermath of these harvest failures, all of them apparently involving groups of more than 50 people. It is not surprising that he talks of the second half of the eighteenth century as the 'golden age of English rioting' (Bohstedt, 1983, *27, 85, 211*).

Reasons for the growth of food rioting

Though some of this chronological increase in the incidence of rioting might be attributable to historians conducting a more intensive scrutiny of the eighteenth century than of earlier periods, and to more events being recorded because of better archival coverage, the scale of the increase is nevertheless such as to suggest that one is dealing with a real rather than an illusory phenomenon. It is hard to conceive that future research into grain rioting will manage to make the 1590s look like the 1790s. A number of factors must have contributed to this tendency for such disturbances to increase, though it is difficult to disentangle and to weight them.

It is generally agreed that these were revolts of consumers rather than food producers, and that prominent parts in these disturbances were played by the inhabitants of market towns and of industrial areas. Thus we should note again that changing balance between food producers and food consumers to which we drew attention at the outset. The ratio of the one to the other increased, especially as population growth resumed briskly in the eighteenth century, and behind this expanding ratio there lurked the growth of towns, the expansion of industrial and service occupations, and, in the agricultural sector, the increasing average size of farms. Not only was more food being marketed, but more consumers were being affected by natural and market fluctuations.

This brings us to that other set of background influences to which attention has been drawn. The increase that took place in marketing was increasingly conducted via private dealings on the farm or in inns, rather than by sales through the public markets. More transactions were being conducted through middlemen dealers, rather than by face to face deals between actual producer and final consumer (Chartres, 1977). A graphic contemporary description of these crucial changes was given by a Lancashire vicar in 1800:

The farmers in this district about twenty years ago were accustomed to take their own corn to market. But this custom has for the last ten or twelve years been wholly discontinued. It is now sold by sample to the corn factor, the regular flourman or the miller-flourman; for the millers have, most of them joined the occupation of flourman to their own, and discover no readiness to grind the corn of the neighbouring inhabitants for their own use, except they happen to be under an obligation to do so, which is seldom the case. Those people buy up all the corn the farmer has to spare, deposit it in their storehouses and pay for it generally when the times approach at which the farmers respectively pay their rents, so that all the grain which the farmer has to dispose of passes at once into the hands of these dealers, and they sell it again when ground in large quantities only, to the retailers in the market, who depend upon them entirely for a regular constant supply; and the housekeeper instead of buying corn of the farmer and sending it to the mill, as heretofore, to be ground for his own use, is under the necessity in most situations of buying his flour at the shop of the retailer. The grain passes from the flourman to the retailer, before it comes in flour into the hands of the consumer. When the flour is sent to market, no business can be done before the respective owners of it arrive, on their arrival they must consult together and fix the price; if there should appear a backwardness in the buyers some of these dealers by their artful conduct, and the ceremony and delay they use in opening the market, have rendered themselves liable to suspicion of procuring people to purchase a quantity at the price they had before fixed among themselves, which continues to be the price of the day. It is painful to suppose that there should be any grounds for such an iniquitous artifice (Cited in Booth, 1977, 92).

Reports of such marketing practices in the south and east of England are to be found at least as early as the sixteenth century, although this report implies that they had only lately made an appearance in Lancashire. Recognition of the essential nature of middlemen in the food trades can be seen in the decline of restrictions on their activity in the later seventeenth and eighteenth centuries.

Signs of the influence of these two sets of developments – an increasing body of consumers and changes in the organisation of marketing – can be discerned in several ways. The characteristic riot of the first half of our period generally involved the seizure of grain in transit by crowds assembled in those market towns of southern England through which grain moved from the corn-producing to corn-consuming regions (Underdown, 1985, *116*). By the second half of the eighteenth century, however, this type of disturbance was being increasingly challenged by attacks on the premises of urban dealers – corn, meal and flour merchants – and on millers. If it was the sight of grain departing from the locality that caused outrage in the sixteenth century, it was more the insufficiency of incoming supplies and the real or supposed iniquities of the sellers that were to do so in the eighteenth century. More and more of these disturbances were also taking place in the towns and expanding industrial regions north of the Trent (Booth, 1977, *89*; Charlesworth, 1983; Stevenson, 1974, *45*).

One must not envisage, however, a situation in which this increasing mass of consumers was automatically triggered into rioting by the shock effects of periodic harvest failure. What has been called the 'spasmodic' view of riotous behaviour is clearly an insufficient explanation (Thompson, 1974, *76*). Even in 1800 only a tiny minority of the population rioted against food prices, and not all of those who had control of the supply of foodstuffs were the targets of attack. It required something more to persuade consumers to act in this concerted and discriminating fashion. Nor was the increased prominence of rioting the consequence, as has been suggested, of an increased frequency of bad harvests (Stevenson, 1974, *39*). The overall frequency of failure in the period 1750–99 was identical to that of the years 1700–49, and, if anything, the first half of the eighteenth century appears to have seen more serious failures than the second half (see Table 1, p. 12).

Changes in patterns of government intervention, however, should be taken into consideration. Intervention in the sixteenth and early seventeenth centuries does appear to have been generally both swift and energetic. Indeed, examples can be found of the executive acting in anticipation of future scarcity (Outhwaite, 1981, *403–4*). With the decline of prompting from central government after the early 1630s, however, initiatives were left with local authorities. Although the crisis of the later 1640s saw local justices busily implementing the old familiar policies, it is likely that from the mid-seventeenth century onwards such local intervention came to be even more patchy than it had been at its height; and central government intervention, as we have argued, tended to become half-hearted and belated. Indeed, in the late eighteenth century explicit *laissez-faire* doctrines were being espoused by some members of the government (Bohstedt, 1983, *61*; Stevenson, 1974, *41–4*; Wells, 1988, *230–48*). The cry of the rioters who seized corn in Oxfordshire in 1693, that 'they were resolved to put the law in execution since the magistrates neglected it', is neither the first nor the last example that can be offered, though it is perhaps the most explicit (Rose, 1961, *280*). Many more riots were terminated by the magistrates making a show of market intervention, than by the authorities suppressing them with force and fear (Bohstedt, 1983, *61*; Thompson, 1974, *403–4*).

It has been suggested also that the characteristic central government interventionist measure of the later period – the invoking of the Edwardian statutes against forestalling, engrossing and regrating – simply served to fuel popular suspicions and public resentments about middlemen, and that these measures may actually have encouraged attacks upon them and their premises. As one mid-eighteenth century writer put it, 'if there is no real want of corn among us, it is certain the present dearness must be owing to the wicked combination of the forestallers, factors, engrossers, badgers, farmers or maltsters' (Barnes, 1930, *33–9*; Shelton, 1973, *46–8*). The repeal in 1772 of all the old anti-middlemen statutes removed the basis for this sort of central intervention, but centuries of prejudice were not so easily swept away, particularly as they were fed from time to time by local prosecutions of offenders under the common law (Bohstedt, 1983, *25, 48*; Rose, 1961, *289–90*; Thompson, 1971, *88*).

The growth in the incidence of food rioting in the eighteenth century appears to have involved two processes: there was a geographical spreading of such disturbances, and there was also an increasing incidence within some districts and communities. The latter may have fed traditions of rioting. 'In Devon', it has been argued, 'the surest predictor of riot in 1801 was riot in 1795' (Bohstedt and Williams, 1988, *21*). Riots are thus offered as an example of 'learned behaviour'. The tendency for disturbances to spread may also have been encouraged by the accounts of such events to be found in newspapers. The latter were certainly criticised for reports 'more likely to extend than suppress the mischief' (Booth, 1977, *102*; Shelton, 1973, *11*). Even without this facility, however, reports were likely to be carried from town to neighbouring town by the normal channels of commerce and communication (Charlesworth and Randall, 1987, *202–3*). A series of disturbances began in Nottingham on 31 August 1800, and then spilled out into the surrounding villages and towns; by 4 September they had reached Derby; the next day the crowd rose in Leicester; between 8 and 10 September trouble reached Coventry, Nuneaton and Ashby-de-la-Zouch (Wells, 1988, *120–5, 180*).

Were there also, in eighteenth-century England, decreasing governmental fears of such riotous behaviour? Although Devon was one of the most riotous counties in England by the end of that century, its ruling classes, we are told, 'did not feel immediately threatened by riot' (Bohstedt, 1983, *27, 58*). By contrast, with limited military resources available, governments in the sixteenth and early seventeenth centuries frequently had the smell of sedition in their nostrils. Riot, Walter argues, 'hinted at the darker nightmare of popular rebellion' (1985, *92*). It is arguable that it was this that lay behind the policies of prompt intervention to assuage popular discontent and the savage punishments meted out to those who swayed too far from the established protocol of riot (Walter, 1980 and 1985). Too much significance should not be ascribed, however, to the growth in the later period of standing armies. Local officials, as we have noted, were frequently reluctant to call in the military, and historians appear to be more impressed by the part the militia played as rioters than they are by their role as policemen (Bohstedt, 1983, *49–50*; Shelton, 1973, *124*; Stevenson, 1974, *47*). Throughout the period as a whole those who took part in these events appear generally to have escaped punishment by legal process. Only persistent or serious offenders were brought before the courts, and not all of these were punished.

The 'moral economy' of the crowd?

The points made so far do not add up to an explanation of why food riots occurred when and where they did. Answers to such questions involve exploration of complex issues relating to social structure and crowd psychology (Bohstedt, 1983 and Wells, 1988 supply the fullest explanation of late eighteenth-century rioting). Those seeking enlightenment should still start, however, with Thompson's justly celebrated essay of 1971 on 'The moral economy of the English crowd in the eighteenth century'. Few articles published in the last twenty years have been as influential.

In this work Thompson laid bare just what it was in the new marketing systems that were developing in the food trades that irked ordinary working people. He was concerned to show that though sharply rising food prices, perhaps hunger, and marketing iniquities were necessary ingredients in any explanation of food rioting, they were not in themselves a sufficient explanatory set. Provoked by a view of rioters as mindless, dearth-programmed automata, he set out to explore the *mentalité* of those directly involved in food disturbances. These rioters were, he felt, articulating a particular set of beliefs. A key passage is:

. . . these grievances operated within a popular consensus as to what were legitimate and what were illegitimate practices in marketing, milling, baking, etc. This in turn was grounded upon a consistent traditional view of social norms and obligations, of the proper economic functions of several parties within the community, which, taken together, can be said to constitute the moral economy of the poor (*79*).

He was impressed by the recurring patterns he saw exhibited in these disturbances, by the disciplined and restrained behaviour of the crowd, and above all by their action of 'setting the price'. Looting was rare. Rioters were more inclined to intimidate farmers or traders into selling at reduced prices, sometimes with the aid of magistrates, or else they seized stocks and sold them themselves, reimbursing the legitimate owners, but at less than market rates. 'What is extraordinary about this pattern', says Thompson, 'is that it reproduces, sometimes with great precision, the emergency measures in time of scarcity whose operation, in the years between 1580 and 1630, were codified in the *Book of Orders*' (*108*).

Few modern essays have had such a powerful historiographical impact: the patterns that Thompson described were quickly replicated by other historians working in the same and earlier centuries. But a number of reservations have also been expressed. The argument hinges essentially on the rioters' possession of a particular ideology, and, it has been pointed out, this has been constructed very largely from the actions of the rioters rather than from their expressed thoughts (Bohstedt, 1983, *35*). Others, whilst accepting the existence of such ideologies, have argued that they were likely to have been more widespread than rioting itself. Thought systems, such as a 'moral economy', cannot explain the geography of rioting (Stevenson, 1974, *67*). Nor can they explain why in a particular community some rioted whilst others did not. The 'crowd', Stevenson reminds us, was not 'a representative section of the common people as a whole' (Stevenson, 1985, *236*). If, moreover, such beliefs were activated by their conjunction with those emerging new commercial tendencies in the food trades, then one should allow that 'The chronologies of food rioting and of capitalist market development do not match' (Bohstedt, 1983, *212*). Doubts have thus been raised about the explanatory value of the concept of the 'moral economy'. But one also needs to examine its specification. Central to it, as we have seen, was the action of 'setting the price'. This should not be equated with the imposition of some sort of ideal or fair price, dimly recalled from the past. The prices that rioters imposed varied in time and space; where they can be measured they turn out often to be near the prices of the previous season (Stevenson, 1974, *64–5*; Bohstedt, 1983, *211*). One can also query the centrality of price-fixing in Tudor and early Stuart market intervention. These policies were much more concerned with ensuring that ordinary purchasers in local markets were served and that surpluses were directed to where the needs were deemed to be greatest. Although there was a threat that prices would be imposed in the *Orders* of 1630, 'price-fixing had been tried back in 1550 and had then proved impracticable' (Slack, 1980a, *4*). Despite all these reservations, however, Thompson's essay repays repeated reading.

5

Some loose ends

This attempt to impose conciseness and coherence on a lengthy set of turbulent and complex events means inevitably that a good many problems have been ignored and qualifications smoothed away. Further reading, particularly of those modern items listed in the bibliography, will inevitably raise doubts about many of the assertions made in this brief work. Much is still unresearched and uncertain, and this chapter wishes to draw attention to just a few of the many problems still outstanding.

By the end of the 250 years covered in this study, England had become less harvest sensitive in at least one important respect. Proportionately fewer people died when the harvests failed. But was there a decisive turning point in this transition? Current opinion, strongly influenced by Appleby's writings, sees 1623 as something of a watershed. It has also been argued that after 1640 the correlation between wheat prices and mortality fell noticeably. Some doubts have already been raised about the latter finding, with Galloway insisting on a closer correlation in the 80 years after 1675 than the long era before this (see above, pp. 20–1). Consideration of individual dearths also raises some doubts, particularly if one takes notice of the observation that 'Only extremely high prices had a contemporaneous (same year) effect on mortality; the peak effect for most price levels was delayed one or two years' (Wrigley and Schofield, 1981, *399*). Appleby himself was prepared to entertain the possibility of a subsistence basis to the severe mortality crisis of 1638/9, induced by the devastation of the barley crop in the harvest year 1637/8 (Appleby, 1978, *191*). The bad harvest of 1678/9 was accompanied by a sharp increase in mortality in 1679. The two successive dearths of 1727/8 and 1728/9 coincided with exceptionally heavy death rates in the years 1727–30, the most severe mortality episode since the mid-sixteenth century. The bad harvests of 1739/40 and 1740/1 were the prelude to the mortality crisis of 1741/2, one ranked eighth in a descending list of crisis mortality years (Wrigley and Schofield, 1981, *333, 532–3, 652–3*). Although there are years of high prices that appeared to coincide with low, and even falling, mortality (such as 1673/4, most of the six poor wheat harvests of the 1690s, and the two bad harvests beginning in 1708 and 1709), enough examples of the reverse sort exist to make one want to question the conclusion that England escaped from subsistence crises by the mid-1620s. Perhaps it would be more accurate to argue that whilst down to about 1640 bad harvests were generally accompanied or succeeded by noticeable worsenings in mortality, in the hundred years that followed, the effects of dearth became less predictable. It was only after the early 1740s that the dearth-death link was decisively broken.

Such a sequence also questions the applicability of many of the explanations that have been offered for the 'disappearance' of subsistence crises by the mid-seventeenth century. Answers to such problems will not be forthcoming until some of these mortality episodes have been subjected to analyses similar to that Post conducted for the early 1740s. The crises of the years 1727–30 call out for further investigation, as do earlier dearths such as 1630/1 and 1661/2 where there are suggestions of rises in numbers of local mortality crises (Dobson, 1987; Gooder, 1972; Outhwaite, 1981). A clearer picture of the disease history of these years will obviously help us to establish how autonomous the death rate really was. Similarly, what was it that helped the population to withstand sequences of disastrous wheat harvests, such as those of 1647/8 to 1649/50, the 1690s, or the two years 1708/9 and 1709/ 10? Although many of these dearths may have precipitated Malthusian preventive checks – falls in nuptiality and fertility – the positive check became much less predictable. Is this element of unpredictability to be explained by the possibility that not all regions achieved immunity at the same time?

As for public policy, whilst we have a reasonably full picture of what was happening at the level of national government, there is a crying need for more work on what was happening in particular local administrations. This would obviously help us to assess the effects of local magisterial intervention, not only in the possible relief of want and misery but also in the relief of unrest. Were there pronounced differences in the willingness of the magistrates to intervene between counties or between towns? What changes took place in the long run? The answers to such questions may help to explain the geography and chronology of riot.

All too little has been said about rioting itself, particularly given the amount that has been written on the subject. Many earlier observations are now being questioned, such as, for example, the significance of the role of women in these disturbances (Bohstedt, 1988). Fuller consideration should perhaps have been given to the forms that food rioting took. We need, however, a clearer taxonomy of food rioting before this can be undertaken with confidence. Although we can no longer accept Rose's view that the earliest example of a price-fixing riot was in 1693, for examples have been found as far back as the sixteenth century, it is still unclear as to when, or if ever, this became a dominating form (Clark, 1976, *379*; Rose, 1961, *279*). Some would argue that such crowd actions only became prominent at the very end of the eighteenth century, that examples of what has been called *taxation populaire* were rare in 1766 but not in 1795 and 1801 (Bohstedt and Williams, 1988, *6*). If this is true, what lay behind it? Can it be linked in any way with changes in public policy? The reimposition of statutory price controls on exports in the Act of 1773 certainly thrust prices and possible price manipulation into the arena of public discussion, perhaps making consumers more price conscious as a consequence. Here is yet another problem that requires investigation. The last word on the complicated interrelationships between dearth, public policies and social disturbances has not been written and probably never will be.

Select bibliography

This list is confined largely to works cited in the text. The inclusion of more of the abundant literature on rioting would have greatly swollen it. Much of this writing can be retrieved via the works of Stevenson and Bohstedt cited below. Citations in the text consist of the author's name, date of publication (sometimes ordered a and b), followed, where necessary, by particular page numbers.

Appleby, A. B. (1973) 'Disease or famine? Mortality in Cumberland and Westmorland, 1580–1640', *Economic History Review*, XXVI, 403–31. Appleby's first thoughts on the dramatic mortality crises that hit the north-west in this period.

Appleby, A. B. (1975) 'Nutrition and Disease: The Case of London, 1550–1750', *Journal of Interdisciplinary History*, 6, 1–22. Needs to be read in conjunction with the works of Galloway and Landers cited below.

Appleby, A. B. (1978) *Famine in Tudor and Stuart England* (Liverpool University Press). Enlarges on his earlier work. Readable and highly influential.

Appleby, A. B. (1979) 'Grain Prices and Subsistence Crises in England and France, 1590–1740', *Journal of Economic History*, XXXIX, 865–87. Offers an intriguing explanation for France's vulnerability to subsistence crises and England's relative immunity.

Ashton, T. S. (1959) *Economic Fluctuations in England 1700–1800* (Oxford: Clarendon Press). A classic account of the economic importance of harvests in eighteenth-century England.

Barnes, D. G. (1930) *A History of the English Corn Laws 1660–1846* (London: George Routledge and Sons). Still an indispensable repository of information on the corn laws, though the interpretation of events needs to be reworked.

Bohstedt, J. (1983) *Riots and Community Politics in England and Wales, 1790–1810* (Cambridge, Mass: Harvard University Press). Important attempt to explain why riots occurred.

Bohstedt, J. (1988) 'Gender, Household and Community Politics: Women in English Riots 1790–1810', *Past and Present*, 120, 88–122. Examines the role of women in rioting and questions the significance traditionally attached to it.

Bohstedt, J. and Williams, D. E. (1988) 'The Diffusion of Riots: The Patterns of 1766, 1795, and 1801 in Devonshire', *Journal of Interdisciplinary History*, XIX, 1–24. An examination of how and why riots spread in one county.

Booth, A. (1977) 'Food Riots in the North-west of England, 1790–1801', *Past and Present*, 77, 84–107. Establishes that the north-west should not be excluded from the history of rioting.

Bowden, P. (1967) 'Agricultural Prices, Farm Profits and Rents', in J. Thirsk (ed.), *The Agrarian History of England and Wales, IV, 1500–1640* (Cambridge University Press). Produces an important statistical appendix on grain prices and an interpreting analysis of their movements in the period 1500 to 1640.

Bowden, P. (1985) 'Agricultural Prices, Wages, Farm Profits and Rents', in J. Thirsk (ed.), *The Agrarian History of England and Wales, V: 2, 1640–1750* (Cambridge University Press). Ditto for the years 1640–1750.

Chambers, J. D. (1972) *Population, Economy and Society in Pre-industrial England* (Oxford University Press). Posthumously published lectures of a pioneer in this field.

Charlesworth, A. (ed.) (1983) *An Atlas of Rural Protest in Britain 1548–1900* (London: Croom Helm). Interesting attempt to map various forms of rioting, not all of which was rural.

Charlesworth, A. and Randall, A. J. (1987) 'Comment: Morals, Markets and the English Crowd in 1766', *Past and Present*, 114, 200–13. A defence of Thompson, 1971.

Chartres, J. A. (1977) *Internal Trade in England 1500–1700* (London: Macmillan). Useful brief survey of trading developments in this period.

Clark, P. (1976) 'Popular Protest and Disturbance in Kent 1558–1640', *Economic History Review*, XXIX, 365–82. Finds Thompson-like patterns in early Kentish riots.

Clark, P. (1983) *The English Alehouse: a Social History* (London: Longman). Scholarly and entertaining account of drinking establishments, and attempts to bring them under control.

Clarkson, L. A. (1975) *Death, Disease and Famine in Pre-industrial England* (Dublin: Gill and Macmillan). Readable, pre-Wrigley and Schofield survey.

Creedy, J. (1986) 'On the King-Davenant "Law" of Demand', *Scottish Journal of Political Economy*, 33, 193–212. Interesting exploration of the mathematical basis, and possible origins, of the formula discussed by Wrigley, 1989.

Dobson, M. J. A. (1987) A Chronology of Epidemic Disease and Mortality in Southeast England, 1601–1800, Historical Geography Research Series, No. 19 (London: Historical Geography Research Group, University College, Nov.). Analyses fluctuations in mortality alongside contemporary comment on illness and disease.

Drake, M. (1962) 'An Elementary Exercise in Parish Register Demography', *Economic History Review*, XIV, 427–45. Mortality crises in the West Riding of Yorkshire.

Everitt, A., (1967) 'The Marketing of Agricultural Produce', in J. Thirsk (ed.), *The Agrarian History of England and Wales, IV, 1500–1640* (Cambridge University Press). The origin of much modern thinking on marketing trends in the early modern period.

Fletcher, A. and Stevenson, J. (1985) *Order and Disorder in Early Modern England* (Cambridge University Press). Useful editorial introduction, and see Stevenson, 1985.

Fletcher, A. (1986) *Reform in the Provinces: the Government of Stuart England* (New Haven: Yale University Press). Useful survey of work on government at various levels.

Flinn, M. W. (1974) 'The Stabilization of Mortality in Pre-industrial Western Europe', *Journal of European Economic History*, 3, 285–318. On the diminution of mortality crises.

Forbes, T. R. (1979) 'By What Disease or Casualty: The Changing Face of Death in London', in C. Webster (ed.), *Health, Medicine and Mortality in the Sixteenth Century* (Cambridge University Press). Anecdotal rather than analytical.

Galloway, P. R. (1985) 'Annual Variations in Death by Age, Deaths by Cause, Prices and Weather in London 1670–1830', *Population Studies*, 39, 487–505. The reverse of Forbes, 1979.

Galloway, P. R. (1988) 'Basic Patterns in Annual Variations in Fertility, Nuptiality, Mortality and Prices in Pre-industrial Europe', *Population Studies*, 42, 275–304. Sophisticated statistical analysis, producing results sometimes at odds with Wrigley and Schofield, 1981.

Gooder, A. (1972) 'The Population Crisis of 1727–30 in Warwickshire', *Midland History*, 1, 1–22. Argues the case for a subsistence element in this major crisis.

Gras, N. S. B. (1915) *The Evolution of the English Corn Market* (Cambridge, Mass.: Harvard University Press). A classic study.

Harrison, C. J. (1971) 'Grain Price Analysis and Harvest Qualities, 1465–1634', *Agricultural History Review*, 19, 135–55. A critique of Hoskins below. Some cautionary remarks in Appleby, 1975.

Heinze, R. W. (1976) *The Proclamations of the Tudor Kings* (Cambridge University Press). Useful on Privy Council intervention before Elizabeth's reign.

Holderness, B. A. (1989) 'Prices, Productivity, and Output', in G. E.

Mingay (ed.), *The Agrarian History of England and Wales, VI, 1750–1850* (Cambridge University Press). Essential reading on these themes.

Hoskins, W. G. (1964, 1968) 'Harvest Fluctuations and English Economic History, 1480–1619', *Agricultural History Review*, 12, 28–46; and 'Harvest Fluctuations and English Economic History, 1620–1759', *Agricultural History Review*, 16, 15–31. An influential application of Beveridge's calculations of wheat prices. See Harrison, 1971.

John, A. H. (1989) 'Statistical Appendix' to G. E. Mingay (ed.), *The Agrarian History of England and Wales, VI, 1750–1850* (Cambridge University Press). Useful statistical source.

Jones, E. L. (1964) *Seasons and Prices* (London: George Allen and Unwin). Astute commentary on seasonality.

Jones, E. L. (ed.) (1967) *Agriculture and Economic Growth in England, 1650–1815* (London: Methuen). Jones here traces important regional shifts in the balance of farming.

Komlos, J. (1988) 'The Food Budget of English Workers: A Comment on Shammas', *Journal of Economic History*, 48, 149. See Shammas, 1983.

Landers, J. (1987) 'Mortality and Metropolis: The Case of London 1625–1825', *Population Studies*, 41, 59–76. Patterns of mortality in London.

Landers, J. and Mouzas, A. (1988) 'Burial Seasonality and Causes of Death in London 1670–1819', *Population Studies*, 42, 59–83. Painstaking exploration of major causes of death in the capital.

Laslett, P. (1965) *The World We Have Lost* (London: Methuen; 3rd edn, 1983). The starting point for much modern discussion of dearth-death relationships.

Lawson, P. (1986) 'Parliament, The Constitution and Corn: The Embargo Crisis of 1766', *Parliamentary History*, 5, 17–37. Explores the politics of suspension of corn exports.

Malcolmson, R. W. (1981) *Life and Labour in England 1700–1780* (London: Hutchinson). Contains useful short section on rioting.

Manning, R. B. (1988) *Village Revolts: Social Protest and Popular Disturbances in England, 1509–1640* (Oxford: Clarendon Press). On enclosure riots.

Mathias, P. (1959) *The Brewing Industry in England 1700–1830* (Cambridge University Press). Classic study but concentrates mostly on production trends.

Outhwaite, R. B. (1978) 'Food Crises in Early Modern England: Patterns of Public Response', in M. W. Flinn (ed.), *Proceedings of the Seventh International Economic History Congress* (Edinburgh University Press). Brief comparison of intervention in 1590s and 1690s.

Outhwaite, R. B. (1981) 'Dearth and Government Intervention in English Grain Markets, 1590–1700', *Economic History Review*, XXXIV, 389–406. Traces abandonment of central government intervention.

Outhwaite, R. B. (1985) 'Dearth, The English Crown and The "Crisis of the 1590s"', in P. Clark (ed.), *The European Crisis of the 1590s* (London: George Allen and Unwin). Explores reasons why successive harvest failure did not have more serious consequences.

Outhwaite, R. B. (1986) 'Progress and Backwardness in English Agriculture, 1500–1650', *Economic History Review*, XXXIX, 1–18. Explores the weaknesses rather than the developing strengths of farming before 1650.

Perren, R. (1989) 'Markets and Marketing', in G. E. Mingay (ed.), *The Agrarian History of England and Wales, VI, 1750–1850* (Cambridge University Press). Has short section on government and dearth measures.

Post, J. D. (1985) *Food Shortage, Climatic Variability and Epidemic Disease in Pre-industrial Europe* (Ithaca, NY: Cornell University Press). Important study of the European-wide crisis of the early 1740s.

Rogers, C. D. (1975) *The Lancashire Population Crisis of 1623* (Manchester University Extra Mural Department). Showed that crisis of 1623 was wider than Laslett thought.

Rose, R. B. (1961) 'Eighteenth Century Price Riots and Public Policy in England', *International Review of Social History*, VI, 277–92. An important early survey of grain rioting.

Rotberg, R. I. and Rabb, T. K. (eds) (1985) *Hunger and History* (Cambridge University Press, 1985). Proceedings of a conference on nutrition-dearth links.

Rudé, G. (1964) *The Crowd in History* (New York: Wiley). Rescues the mob from anonymity.

Schofield, R. S. (1985) 'The Impact of Scarcity and Plenty on Population Change in England, 1541–1871', in Rotberg and Rabb. Retrieves some important ideas from Wrigley and Schofield, 1981.

Scrimshaw, N. S., Taylor, C. E. and Gordon, J. E. (1968) *Interactions of Nutrition and Infection* (World Health Organization, Geneva). Authoritative general survey of medical evidence. But see Rotberg and Rabb, 1985.

Shammas, C. (1983) 'Food Expenditure and Well-being', *Journal of Economic History*, 43, 89–100. Underlines how little we really know about diets, especially in the early modern period.

Sharp, B. (1980) *In Contempt of all Authority* (London: University of California Press). Explores rioting in the west of England, 1586–1660.

Shelton, W. J. (1973) *English Hunger and Industrial Disorders* (London: Macmillan). The riots of 1766.

Slack, P. (1979) 'Mortality Crises and Epidemic Disease in England 1485–1610', in C. Webster (ed.), *Health, Medicine and Mortality in the Sixteenth Century* (Cambridge University Press). A pre-Wrigley and Schofield general survey, but well worth reading.

Slack, P. (1980a) 'Books of Orders: The Making of English Social Policy, 1575–1631', *Transactions of the Royal Historical Society*, fifth series, 30, 1–22. Important study of the development of this device.

Slack, P. (1980b) 'Social Policy and the Constraints of Government, 1547–58', in J. Loach and R. Tittler (eds), *The Mid-Tudor Polity, c. 1540–1560* (Basingstoke: Macmillan Education). For government intervention in the mid-Tudor period.

Slack, P. (1988) *Poverty and Policy in Tudor and Stuart England* (London: Longman). Authoritative general survey of poverty and its relief.

Stevenson, J. (1974) 'Food Riots in England, 1792–1818', in R. Quinault and J. Stevenson (eds), *Popular Protest and Public Order* (London: George Allen and Unwin). The first of Stevenson's two important surveys of food rioting.

Stevenson, J. (1979) *Popular Disturbances in England 1700–1870* (London: Longman). Traces the history of rioting generally.

Stevenson, J. (1985) 'The "Moral Economy" of the English Crowd: Myth and Reality', in A. Fletcher and J. Stevenson (eds), *Order and Disorder in Early Modern England* (Cambridge University Press). Stevenson develops his critique of Thompson.

Thirsk, J. (1961) 'Industries in the Countryside', in F. J. Fisher (ed.), *Essays in the Economic and Social History of Tudor and Stuart England* (Cambridge University Press). Drew attention to the structure of and developments in wood-pasture regions.

Thirsk, J. (1985) 'Agricultural Policy: Public Debate and Legislation', in J. Thirsk (ed.), *The Agrarian History of England and Wales, V.2, 1640–1750* (Cambridge University Press). Essential, wide-ranging discussion.

Thirsk, J. and Cooper, J. P. (1972) *Seventeenth Century Economic Documents* (Oxford: Clarendon Press). Documents illustrating the nature of intervention.

Thompson, E. P. (1971) 'The Moral Economy of the English Crowd in the Eighteenth Century', *Past and Present*, 50, 76–136. Established the framework for discussion for a generation.

Thompson, E. P. (1974) 'Patrician Society, Plebeian Culture', *Journal of Social History*, 7, 382–405. Extends the ideas expressed earlier.

Underdown, D. (1985) *Revel, Riot and Rebellion* (Oxford University Press). Readable attempt to integrate the social structure and politics of differing regions in Somerset before 1660.

Walter, J. (1980) 'Grain Riots and Popular Attitudes to the Law', in J. Brewer and J. Styles (eds), *An Ungovernable People* (London:

Hutchinson). Draws out the general significance of events at Maldon in 1629.

Walter, J. (1985) 'A "Rising of the People"? The Oxfordshire Rising of 1596', *Past and Present*, 107, 90–143. Explores an abortive rebellion.

Walter, J. (1989) 'The Social Economy of Dearth in Early Modern England', in J. Walter and R. Schofield (eds), *Famine, Disease and the Social Order in Early Modern Society* (Cambridge University Press). Rich and imaginative discussion of how people survived.

Walter, J. and Schofield, R. (eds) (1989) *Famine, Disease and the Social Order in Early Modern Society* (Cambridge University Press). A stimulating set of essays, prefaced by a magnificent wide-ranging introduction.

Walter, J. and Wrightson, K. (1976) 'Dearth and the Social Order in Early Modern England', *Past and Present*, 71, 22–42. Puts dearth into its ideological context.

Wells, R. A. (1978) 'Counting Riots in Eighteenth Century England', *Bulletin of the Society for the Study of Labour History*, 37, 68–72. Why it is difficult.

Wells, R. A. (1988) *Wretched Faces: Famine in Wartime England 1793–1801* (Gloucester: Alan Sutton). A richly detailed discussion of the riots of 1795–6 and 1800–1, and their probable causes. Opinions on the work of other scholars (Wrigley and Schofield especially) tend to be vented with the sound and fury appropriate to an eighteenth-century rioter.

Wrigley, E. A. (1986) 'Urban Growth and Agricultural Change', in R. I. Rotberg and T. K. Rabb (eds), *Population and Economy* (Cambridge University Press). Some measures of urbanization.

Wrigley, E. A. (1989) 'Some Reflections on Corn Yields and Prices in Pre-industrial Economies', in J. Walter and R. Schofield. Stimulating reflections on the Davenant quantity-price relationships.

Wrigley, E. A. and Schofield, R. (1981) *The Population History of England, 1541–1871* (London: Edward Arnold). Essential but difficult work. Not the last word on this subject.

Index

Westmorland 21, 23
Whitgift, Archbishop 2–3, 6
Wiltshire 35, 40
World Health Organization Report
   17
Wrightson, K. 38

Wrigley, E. A. 2, 8, 11, 18–19, 22,
   24–5

yields, *see* corn
Yorkshire 2

New Studies in Economic and Social History

Titles in the series available from Cambridge University Press:

Previously published as

Studies in Economic History

Titles in the series available from the Macmillan Press Limited

Economic History Society

The Economic History Society, which numbers around 3,000 members, publishes the *Economic History Review* four times a year (free to members) and holds an annual conference. Enquiries about membership should be addressed to

The Assistant Secretary
Economic History Society
PO Box 70
Kingswood
Bristol
BS15 5TB

Full-time students may join at special rates.